LOW CARB

p

This is a Parragon Book
This edition published in 2005

Parragon
Queen Street House
4 Queen Street
Bath BA1 1HE, UK

ISBN: 1-40544-858-X

Printed in China

Produced by the Bridgewater Book Company Ltd.

NOTE

This book uses metric and imperial measurements. Follow the same
units of measurement throughout; do not mix metric and imperial.
All spoon measurements are level: teaspoons are assumed to be 5 ml,
and tablespoons are assumed to be 15 ml. Unless otherwise stated,
milk is assumed to be full fat, eggs and individual vegetables such as
potatoes are medium, and pepper is freshly ground black pepper.

The times given for each recipe are an approximate guide
only because the cooking times may vary as a result of the
types of oven and other equipment used.

Recipes using raw or very lightly cooked eggs should be
avoided by infants, the elderly, pregnant women, convalescents and
anyone suffering from an illness. Pregnant and breast-feeding women
are advised to avoid eating peanuts and peanut products.

Contents

Introduction

What constitutes a healthy diet? In one way, the answer to this question is very straightforward, while in another, it is almost impossible. It is true that a balanced intake of all the various food groups – fats, proteins and carbohydrates – in their appropriate proportions is the ideal that  nutritionists encourage us to aim for. However, this raises a number of questions: where we are starting from, how old we are, what kind of lives we lead, whether we are men or women and even how to estimate a 'balanced intake' and 'appropriate proportions'. For various reasons, many of us have allowed the extra weight to creep on and developed eating patterns that, at best, do our bodies no favours and, at worst, make us sluggish, fat, unhappy and ill. A low-carbohydrate diet is one very successful way of tackling these sorts of problems, revitalizing and re-energizing the system and trimming off the spare tyre around the tummy.

What are carbohydrates?

The name of this food group derives from the chemical elements it contains – carbon, hydrogen and oxygen – which form compounds such as starch and sugars. When these are eaten, the body breaks them down to release energy. They are found in a wide variety of commonly eaten foods. Grains and cereals, for example, feature in most meals, from the morning's cornflakes, through the lunchtime sandwich, to the evening plate of pasta. Potatoes are a starchy staple and pulses, such as peas and beans, are also high in carbohydrates. Many popular snacks – chocolate bars, biscuits, muffins, doughnuts and fizzy drinks – are packed with sugars. Carbohydrates are comfort foods, making us feel full and satisfied.

There is a second type of carbohydrate that our bodies cannot digest and this is usually called dietary fibre. This contributes to the feeling of fullness after a meal and helps to regulate the digestive system, but the body cannot break it down to release energy. This kind of carbohydrate is found in wheat bran, fruit, pulses, nuts and leafy green vegetables.

Energy and body weight

The body needs energy to function and it obtains this from the food consumed. Even the process of digestion uses up energy. However, the amount of energy you require depends on a number of factors. It is obvious that an Olympic athlete requires more input than a sedentary office worker, but age is also a consideration as the metabolism begins to slow down from about the age of 30. Body type, including the amount of muscle mass and lean tissue, also affects energy requirements.

Energy is measured as calories, also called kilocalories (kcal), and as kilojoules (kJ). 1 kcal equals about 4 kJ. Many of the calories consumed are used quite quickly for everyday activities, from breathing to walking up the stairs. The energy that is not used is converted by the body to be stored in the muscles or as fat. It is easy to see that if you consume more calories than you use, the body will build up a store of fat.

The following is a guide to the approximate daily calorie intake required by men and women at different stages in life.

daily calorie intake

Growing children
Boys and girls – 1,800–2,220 calories per day

Adults who exercise/have physical jobs
Men – 2,850 calories per day
Women – 2,150 calories per day

Adults who do not exercise/have sedentary jobs
Men – 2,400 calories per day
Women – 2,000 calories per day

Over 50s
Men – 2,200 calories per day
Women – 1,850 calories per day

How a low-carbohydrate diet can help

Carbohydrates are the main source of energy in our diets, with fats the second most important, so if you want to lose weight, reducing the intake of carbohydrates is a good way to do it. However, cutting them out altogether is neither sensible nor practical, because you will also be cutting out important nutrients. It is also unwise to embark on a drastic reduction of carbohydrates all at once. If you introduce this new eating pattern gradually, you will not encounter the mood swings or hunger pangs that so often go with attempts to diet and usually result in failure.

While it is true that taking in more energy than is expended is the reason why fat accumulates in the body, individual metabolism also plays a part. Some people are simply more intolerant of carbohydrates than others and can almost see their hips growing with every slice of bread. Pay attention to your body and respond to its particular requirements.

Previously, the most difficult aspect of a low-carbohydrate diet was deciding what to eat, not what to leave out. This is because much of the variety and contrast in our 'normal' meals is derived from incorporating carbohydrates. Who wants a burger without a bun, steak without chips or meatballs without spaghetti? This problem is now solved because this book provides a wealth of recipes for delicious, low-carbohydrate dishes that are easy to make and will also satisfy the appetite. All the thinking, planning and calorie counting has been done for you. The recipes, based on meat, poultry, eggs, cheese and vegetables, offer both variety and enjoyment.

For many people, a low-carbohydrate diet is a lifetime choice, used to maintain their optimum body weight. Others find it a quick way to shed a few pounds before a summer holiday or after an over-indulgent Christmas. The choice is, of course, personal, but do bear in mind that if you return to higher carbohydrate meals, you are likely to regain the weight.

Choosing low-carbohydrate ingredients

Labels providing nutritional information on packaged foods are not always as clear and helpful as they might be. However, carbohydrate content is normally included and covers both starches and sugars. Dietary fibre, non-digestible carbohydrate, is usually listed separately. Not all products include a measure of fibre, either because there isn't any or because figures are not available. If you take a calculator shopping with you, you may find it helpful to know that 1 gram of carbohydrate supplies about 3.75 calories or 16 kilojoules of energy.

There is no reason why you shouldn't substitute one ingredient for another in any of the recipes in this book, provided that it does not increase the carbohydrate count. While Brie contains only traces of carbohydrate, Stilton may have 2 grams per 100 grams – a small difference, but it will increase the carbohydrate count. Cauliflower contains almost twice as much carbohydrate as broccoli. Also, bear in mind that some most unexpected foods, including many accompaniments and drinks, contain carbohydrates. These will contribute to the overall count. It's no good cooking a low-carbohydrate curry and serving it with a high-carbohydrate chutney. At the same time, there is no point in being obsessive. English mustard may contain about 19 grams of carbohydrate per 100 ml, but when did you last eat more than about ½ teaspoon at one sitting?

Nowadays, there are some specially manufactured low-carbohydrate products on the market, but they are often quite expensive and their labels require very close scrutiny. Jams and spreads produced without added sugar will contain some natural fruit sugars but are generally a good buy. Low-carbohydrate baked goods may be life-savers for the incorrigibly sweet-toothed, but they do vary in quality, while sugar-free sweets and chocolates, originally produced for diabetes sufferers, have a good reputation. Other products may boast of a low-carbohydrate count per portion, but you need to check what the manufacturers regard as a portion – sometimes it's risibly small.

Soups & Starters

Soups are an invaluable part of a healthy low-carbohydrate eating plan, with their comforting and satisfying qualities. They also offer a wide variety of flavours and textures, as the following recipes show. Choose from a smooth vegetable soup, such as Cream of Artichoke Soup (see page 10), or a classic Bouillabaisse (see page 26) with chunks of delicious seafood. For something to really tickle the taste buds, try the Mexican-inspired Chicken, Avocado & Chipotle Soup (see page 22).

Tasty and nutritious vegetables also feature highly in the range of starters on offer – cool, clean-tasting cucumbers in Tsatziki (see page 37), succulent mushrooms in a Soufflé Omelette (see page 46) and sweetly smoky aubergine in the elegant Aubergine Rolls (see page 45). Otherwise, you can major on serious high-protein savouries, such as Bang-Bang Chicken (see page 58).

cream of artichoke soup

serves six

750 g/1 lb 10 oz Jerusalem
   artichokes
1 lemon, thickly sliced
55 g/2 oz butter or margarine
2 onions, chopped
1 garlic clove, crushed
1.3 litres/2¼ pints vegetable stock
salt and pepper
2 bay leaves
¼ tsp ground mace or
   ground nutmeg
1 tbsp lemon juice
150 ml/5 fl oz single cream or
   natural fromage frais
TO GARNISH
roughly grated carrot
chopped fresh parsley or coriander

NUTRITION

Calories 190	Sugars 0g
Protein 0.4g	Fat 2g
Carbohydrate 0.7g	Saturates 0.7g

1 Peel and slice the artichokes. Place in a bowl of water with the lemon slices.

2 Melt the butter in a large saucepan. Add the onions and garlic and fry gently for 3–4 minutes, or until soft but not coloured.

3 Drain the artichokes, discarding the lemon, and add to the saucepan. Mix well and cook gently for 2–3 minutes without allowing to colour.

4 Add the stock, salt and pepper, bay leaves, mace and lemon juice. Bring slowly to the boil, then cover and simmer for 30 minutes, or until the vegetables are very tender.

5 Remove and discard the bay leaves. Cool the soup slightly, then press through a sieve into a bowl. Alternatively, process in a blender or food processor until smooth. If liked, a little of the soup may be only partially puréed and added to the rest of the puréed soup, to give extra texture.

6 Pour into a clean saucepan and bring to the boil. Adjust the seasoning if necessary and stir in the cream. Reheat gently without boiling.

7 Ladle the soup into individual serving bowls, garnish with grated carrot and chopped parsley and serve immediately.

gazpacho

serves four

½ small cucumber

½ small green pepper, deseeded
  and very finely chopped

500 g/1 lb 2 oz ripe tomatoes,
  peeled, or 400 g/14 oz canned
  chopped tomatoes

½ onion, roughly chopped

2–3 garlic cloves, crushed

3 tbsp olive oil

2 tbsp white wine vinegar

1–2 tbsp lemon or lime juice

2 tbsp tomato purée

450 ml/16 fl oz tomato juice

salt and pepper

TO SERVE

chopped green pepper

thinly sliced onion rings

croûtons

NUTRITION

Calories 140	Sugars 12g
Protein 3g	Fat 9g
Carbohydrate 13g	Saturates 1g

1 Roughly grate the cucumber into a large bowl and add the chopped green pepper.

2 Place the tomatoes, onion and garlic in a food processor or blender. Add the oil, vinegar, lemon juice and tomato purée, and process until smooth. Alternatively, finely chop the tomatoes and finely grate the onion, then mix together. Add the crushed garlic, oil, vinegar, lemon juice and tomato purée and mix well.

3 Add the tomato mixture to the bowl and mix well, then add the tomato juice and mix again.

4 Season to taste with salt and pepper, cover and leave to chill for 6 hours, or preferably longer to allow the flavours to meld together.

5 Prepare the side dishes of chopped pepper, thinly sliced onion rings and croûtons, and arrange them in serving bowls. Ladle the soup into cold bowls, handing round the side dishes separately.

chicken consommé

serves eight–ten

1.7 litres/3 pints chicken stock

150 ml/5 fl oz medium sherry

4 egg whites, plus egg shells

salt and pepper

115 g/4 oz cooked chicken,
   thinly sliced

COOK'S TIP

Consommé is usually garnished
with freshly cooked pasta
shapes, noodles, rice or lightly
cooked vegetables. For a low-
carbohydrate option, you could
garnish it with omelette strips,
drained first on kitchen paper.

NUTRITION

Calories 96	Sugars 1g
Protein 11g	Fat 1g
Carbohydrate 1g	Saturates 0.4g

1 Place the stock and sherry in a large, heavy-based saucepan and heat gently for 5 minutes.

2 Add the egg whites and the egg shells to the stock and whisk until the mixture begins to boil.

3 Remove the saucepan from the heat and allow the mixture to subside for 10 minutes. Repeat this heating and subsiding process 3 times. This allows the egg white to trap the sediments in the stock to clarify the soup. Leave the consommé to cool for 5 minutes.

4 Carefully place a piece of fine muslin over a clean saucepan. Ladle the soup over the muslin and sieve into the saucepan.

5 Repeat this process twice, then gently reheat the consommé. Season to taste with salt and pepper, then add the cooked chicken slices. Pour the soup into a warmed serving dish or individual serving bowls.

6 Garnish with any of the suggestions in the Cook's Tip and serve.

crab & ginger soup

serves four

1 carrot, chopped

1 leek, chopped

1 bay leaf

850 ml/1½ pints fish stock

2 medium-sized cooked crabs

2.5-cm/1-inch piece fresh root
    ginger, grated

1 tsp light soy sauce

½ tsp ground star anise

salt and pepper

NUTRITION

Calories 145	Sugars 2.4g
Protein 40g	Fat 5.7g
Carbohydrate 2.7g	Saturates 2.6g

1 Place the carrot, leek, bay leaf and stock into a large saucepan and bring to the boil over a medium heat. Reduce the heat, cover and leave to simmer for 10 minutes, or until the vegetables are nearly tender.

2 Meanwhile, remove the meat from the cooked crabs. Break off the claws, break the joints and remove the meat (you may need a fork or skewer for this). Add the crabmeat to the stock in the saucepan.

3 Add the ginger, soy sauce and star anise to the stock and bring to the boil. Reduce the heat and leave to simmer for 10 minutes, or until the vegetables are tender and the crab is heated through. Season to taste with salt and pepper.

4 Ladle the soup into 4 warmed serving bowls and garnish with crab claws. Serve immediately.

COOK'S TIP

To prepare cooked crab, loosen the meat from the shell by banging the back of the underside with a clenched fist. Stand the crab on its edge with the shell towards you. Force the shell from the body with your thumbs. Twist off the legs and claws and remove the meat. Twist off the tail and discard. Remove and discard the gills from each side of the body. Cut the body in half along the centre and remove the meat. Scoop the brown meat from the shell.

COOK'S TIP

If fresh crabmeat is unavailable, use drained canned crabmeat or thawed frozen crabmeat instead.

fish soup with wontons

serves four

125 g/4½ oz large cooked
    peeled prawns
1 tsp snipped fresh chives, plus
    extra to garnish
1 small garlic clove, finely chopped
1 tbsp vegetable oil
12 wonton wrappers
1 small egg, beaten
850 ml/1½ pints fish stock
175 g/6 oz white fish fillet, diced
dash of chilli sauce
1 fresh red chilli, sliced, to garnish

NUTRITION

Calories 115	Sugars 0g
Protein 16g	Fat 5g
Carbohydrate 1g	Saturates 1g

VARIATION

You can replace the prawns with
cooked crabmeat for an
alternative flavour.

1 Roughly chop a quarter of the prawns and mix together with the snipped chives and garlic.

2 Heat the oil in a preheated wok or large, heavy-based frying pan until it is really hot.

3 Stir-fry the prawn mixture for 1–2 minutes. Remove from the heat and leave to cool completely.

4 Spread out the wonton wrappers on a work surface. Spoon a little of the prawn filling into the centre of each wrapper. Brush the edges of the wrappers with beaten egg and press the edges together, scrunching them to form a 'moneybag' shape. Reserve while you are preparing the soup.

5 Pour the stock into a large saucepan and bring to the boil. Add the fish and the remaining prawns and cook for 5 minutes.

6 Add chilli sauce to taste, then add the wontons and cook for a further 5 minutes.

7 Spoon into warmed bowls, garnish with the sliced chilli and extra snipped chives and serve.

hot & sour soup

serves four

350 g/12 oz whole raw prawns
in shells
1 tbsp vegetable oil
1 lemon grass stalk,
roughly chopped
2 kaffir lime leaves, shredded
1 fresh green chilli, deseeded
and chopped
1.2 litres/2 pints chicken or
fish stock
1 lime
1 tbsp Thai fish sauce
salt and pepper
1 fresh red bird's eye chilli,
deseeded and thinly sliced
1 spring onion, thinly sliced
1 tbsp finely chopped fresh
coriander, to garnish

NUTRITION

Calories 71	Sugars 0g
Protein 8g	Fat 4g
Carbohydrate 1g	Saturates 0g

1 Peel the prawns and reserve the shells. Cut a slit along the back of each prawn and remove the black vein, then place in a bowl, cover and chill.

2 Heat the oil in a large, heavy-based saucepan. Add the prawn shells and stir-fry for 3–4 minutes, or until they turn pink. Add the lemon grass, lime leaves, chilli and stock. Pare a thin strip of rind from the lime and grate the rest. Add the grated rind to the saucepan.

3 Bring to the boil, then reduce the heat, cover and leave to simmer for 20 minutes.

4 Sieve the liquid and pour it back into the saucepan. Squeeze the juice from the lime and add to the saucepan with the fish sauce and salt and pepper to taste.

5 Bring to the boil, then reduce the heat and add the prawns. Simmer for 2–3 minutes.

6 Add the thinly sliced chilli and spring onion. Sprinkle with the lime rind strip and coriander and serve.

spinach & tofu soup

serves four

225 g/8 oz firm tofu
(drained weight)
125 g/4½ oz fresh spinach leaves
700 ml/1¼ pints water or
vegetable stock
1 tbsp light soy sauce
salt and pepper

COOK'S TIP

Soup is an integral part of a
Chinese meal; it is usually
presented in a large bowl placed
in the centre of the table, and
consumed as the meal
progresses. It serves as a
refresher between different
dishes and as a beverage
throughout the meal.

NUTRITION

Calories 33	Sugar 1g
Protein 4g	Fat 2g
Carbohydrate 1g	Saturates 0.2g

1 Using a sharp knife to avoid squashing it, cut the tofu into small cubes about 5 mm/¼ inch thick.

2 Rinse the spinach leaves thoroughly under cold running water and drain well.

3 Cut the spinach leaves into small pieces or shreds, discarding any discoloured leaves and tough stalks. (If possible, use fresh young spinach leaves, which have not yet developed tough ribs. Otherwise, it is important to cut out all the ribs and stems for this soup.) Reserve the spinach until required.

4 Bring the water to a rolling boil in a preheated wok or large, heavy-based frying pan.

5 Add the tofu and soy sauce, return to the boil and simmer for 2 minutes over a medium heat.

6 Add the spinach and simmer for a further minute, stirring gently. Skim the surface of the soup to make it clear and season to taste with salt and pepper.

7 Transfer the soup to a warmed soup tureen or warmed individual serving bowls and serve with chopsticks and a broad, shallow spoon.

chicken soup with almonds

serves four

1 large or 2 small skinless, boneless
   chicken breasts
1 tbsp sunflower oil
4 spring onions, thinly sliced
   diagonally
1 carrot, cut into julienne strips
700 ml/1¼ pints chicken stock
finely grated rind of ½ lemon
40 g/1½ oz ground almonds
1 tbsp light soy sauce
1 tbsp lemon juice
salt and pepper
25 g/1 oz flaked almonds, toasted

NUTRITION

Calories 219	Sugars 2g
Protein 18g	Fat 15g
Carbohydrate 2g	Saturates 2g

1 Cut each chicken breast into 4 strips lengthways, then slice very thinly across the grain to give shreds of meat.

2 Heat the oil in a preheated wok, swirling it around until really hot.

3 Add the spring onions and cook for 2 minutes, then add the chicken and toss it for 3–4 minutes, or until sealed and almost cooked through, stirring constantly. Add the carrot strips and stir well.

4 Add the stock to the wok and bring to the boil. Add the lemon rind, ground almonds, soy sauce, lemon juice and plenty of salt and pepper. Return to the boil and leave to simmer, uncovered, for 5 minutes, stirring occasionally.

5 Adjust the seasoning if necessary, add most of the toasted almonds and continue to cook for a further 1–2 minutes.

6 Serve the soup hot, in individual serving bowls, sprinkled with the remaining toasted almonds.

COOK'S TIP

To toast flaked almonds, place them in a dry frying pan over a medium heat and stir until lightly browned. Keep a close eye on them because they burn very easily.

chicken, avocado & chipotle soup

serves four

1.5 litres/2¾ pints chicken stock

2–3 garlic cloves, finely chopped

1–2 dried chipotle chillies, cut into
very thin strips (see Cook's Tip)

1 avocado

lime or lemon juice, for tossing

3–5 spring onions, thinly sliced

350–400 g/12–14 oz cooked
chicken breast meat, torn or cut
into shreds or thin strips

2 tbsp chopped fresh coriander

TO SERVE

1 lime, cut into wedges

handful of tortilla chips (optional)

NUTRITION

Calories 216	Sugars 1g
Protein 28g	Fat 11g
Carbohydrate 2g	Saturates 2g

VARIATION

Add 400 g/14 oz canned, drained
chickpeas to the bowls with the
spring onions, chicken, avocado
and coriander.

1 Place the stock in a large, heavy-based saucepan with the garlic
and chillies and bring to the boil.

2 Meanwhile, cut the avocado in half around the stone. Twist
apart, then remove the stone with a
knife. Carefully peel off the skin, dice
the flesh and toss in lime juice to
prevent discoloration.

3 Arrange the spring onions, chicken, avocado and coriander in
the base of 4 soup bowls or in a large
serving bowl.

4 Ladle hot stock over and serve with lime wedges and a handful
of tortilla chips, if wished.

COOK'S TIP

Chipotle chillies are smoked and
dried jalapeño chillies. They are
available canned or dried from
specialist shops. They add a
distinctive smoky flavour to
dishes and are very hot. Use
chipotles canned in adobo
marinade for this recipe, if
possible. Drain the canned
version before using. Dried
chipotles need to be
reconstituted before using.

chilli & watercress soup

serves four

1 tbsp sunflower oil

250 g/9 oz smoked tofu
(drained weight), sliced

85 g/3 oz shiitake mushrooms,
sliced

2 tbsp chopped fresh coriander

125 g/4½ oz watercress

1 fresh red chilli, deseeded and
finely sliced, to garnish

STOCK

1 tbsp tamarind pulp

2 dried red chillies, chopped

2 kaffir lime leaves, torn in half

2.5-cm/1-inch piece fresh root
ginger, chopped

5-cm/2-inch piece galangal,
chopped

1 stalk lemon grass, chopped

1 onion, quartered

1 litre/1¾ pints cold water

NUTRITION	
Calories 90	Sugars 1g
Protein 7g	Fat 6g
Carbohydrate 2g	Saturates 1g

1 Place all the ingredients for the stock in a saucepan and bring to the boil.

2 Simmer the stock for 5 minutes. Remove the saucepan from the heat and sieve, reserving the stock.

3 Heat the oil in a preheated wok or large, heavy-based frying pan. Add the tofu and cook over a high heat for 2 minutes, stirring constantly so that the tofu cooks evenly on both sides. Add the sieved stock to the frying pan.

4 Add the mushrooms and coriander and boil for 3 minutes.

5 Add the watercress and boil for a further minute. Serve, garnished with red chilli slices.

VARIATION

You might like to try a mixture of different types of mushroom. Oyster, button and straw mushrooms are all suitable.

24

spinach & ginger soup

serves four

2 tbsp sunflower oil

1 onion, chopped

2 garlic cloves, finely chopped

2.5-cm/1-inch piece fresh root
   ginger, finely chopped

250 g/9 oz fresh young spinach
   leaves

1 small lemon grass stalk,
   finely chopped

1 litre/1¾ pints chicken or
   vegetable stock

1 small potato, chopped

1 tbsp rice wine or dry sherry

salt and pepper

1 tsp sesame oil

NUTRITION

Calories 38	Sugars 0.8g
Protein 3.2g	Fat 1.8g
Carbohydrate 2.4g	Saturates 0.2g

1 Heat the oil in a large saucepan. Add the onion, garlic and ginger and stir-fry gently for 3–4 minutes, or until softened but not browned.

2 Reserve 2–3 small spinach leaves. Add the remaining leaves and lemon grass to the saucepan, stirring until the spinach is wilted. Add the stock and potato to the saucepan and bring to the boil. Reduce the heat, cover and simmer for 10 minutes.

3 Transfer the soup to a food processor or blender and process until completely smooth.

4 Return the soup to the saucepan and add the rice wine, then season to taste with salt and pepper. Heat until just about to boil.

VARIATION

To make a creamy-textured spinach and coconut soup, stir in 4 tablespoons creamed coconut, or replace 300 ml/10 fl oz of the stock with coconut milk. Serve the soup with fresh coconut shavings sprinkled on the top.

5 Finely shred the reserved spinach leaves and sprinkle some over the top. Drizzle with a few drops of sesame oil and serve hot, garnished with the remaining finely shredded spinach leaves.

bouillabaisse

serves six–eight

450 g/1 lb Mediterranean prawns

750 g/1 lb 10 oz firm white fish
　　fillets, such as sea bass, snapper
　　or monkfish

4 tbsp olive oil

grated rind of 1 orange

1 large garlic clove, finely chopped

½ tsp chilli paste or harissa

1 fennel bulb, finely chopped

1 large onion, finely chopped

225 g/8 oz potatoes, halved and
　　thinly sliced

250 g/9 oz scallops

salt and pepper

STOCK

1 large leek, sliced

1 onion, halved and sliced

1 red pepper, deseeded and sliced

3–4 tomatoes, cored and cut
　　into 8 wedges

4 garlic cloves, sliced

1 bay leaf

pinch of saffron threads

½ tsp fennel seeds

600 ml/1 pint water

1.2 litres/2 pints fish stock

1　Peel the prawns and reserve the shells. Cut the fish fillets into pieces about 5 cm/2 inches square. Trim off any ragged edges and reserve. Place the fish in a bowl with 2 tablespoons of the oil, the orange rind, garlic and chilli paste. Turn to coat well, cover and chill the prawns and fish separately.

2　Heat 1 tablespoon of the oil in a large saucepan over a medium heat. Add the leek, sliced onion and red pepper. Cover and cook for 5 minutes, stirring, or until the onion softens. Stir in the tomatoes, sliced garlic, bay leaf, saffron, fennel seeds, prawn shells, fish trimmings, water and fish stock. Bring to the boil, then simmer, covered, for 30 minutes. Sieve the stock.

3　Heat the remaining oil in a separate large saucepan. Add the fennel and chopped onion and cook for 5 minutes until softened. Add the stock and potatoes and bring to the boil. Reduce the heat slightly, cover and cook for 12–15 minutes, or until tender.

4　Reduce the heat and add the fish, thick pieces first and thinner ones after 2–3 minutes. Add the prawns and scallops and leave to simmer until all the seafood is cooked and opaque throughout.

5　Taste and adjust the seasoning if necessary. Ladle into warmed bowls and serve.

NUTRITION	
Calories 273	Sugars 4g
Protein 36g	Fat 9g
Carbohydrate 13g	Saturates 2g

celeriac, leek & potato soup

serves four–six

1 tbsp butter

1 onion, chopped

2 large leeks, halved lengthways
   and sliced

1 large celeriac (about 750 g/1 lb
   10 oz), peeled and diced

1 potato, diced

1 carrot, quartered and thinly sliced

1.2 litres/2 pints water

⅛ tsp dried marjoram

1 bay leaf

salt and pepper

freshly grated nutmeg

celery leaves, to garnish

NUTRITION

Calories 81	Sugars 5g
Protein 3g	Fat 3g
Carbohydrate 11g	Saturates 2g

1 Melt the butter in a large saucepan over a medium heat. Add the onion and leeks and cook for 4 minutes, stirring frequently, or until just softened but not coloured.

2 Add the celeriac, potato, carrot, water, marjoram, bay leaf and a large pinch of salt. Bring to the boil, reduce the heat, cover and leave to simmer for 25 minutes, or until the vegetables are tender. Remove and discard the bay leaf.

3 Leave the soup to cool slightly. Transfer to a food processor or blender and process until smooth. (If using a food processor, sieve off the cooking liquid and reserve. Process the soup solids, moistened with a little cooking liquid, then combine with the remaining liquid.)

4 Return the soup to a clean saucepan and stir to blend. Season to taste with salt, pepper and nutmeg. Stir constantly until reheated.

5 Ladle the soup into warmed soup bowls, garnish with celery leaves and serve.

leek, potato & bacon soup

serves four–six

2 tbsp butter

175 g/6 oz potatoes, diced

4 leeks, shredded

2 garlic cloves, crushed

100 g/3½ oz smoked bacon, diced

850 ml/1½ pints vegetable stock

225 ml/8 fl oz double cream

2 tbsp chopped fresh parsley

salt and pepper

TO GARNISH

vegetable oil

1 leek, shredded

NUTRITION	
Calories 316	Sugars 3g
Protein 11g	Fat 27g
Carbohydrate 9g	Saturates 15g

1 Melt the butter in a large saucepan. Add the potatoes, leeks, garlic and bacon and sauté gently for 5 minutes, stirring constantly.

2 Add the stock and bring to the boil. Reduce the heat, cover and leave to simmer for 20 minutes, or until the potatoes are cooked. Stir in the double cream and mix well.

3 Meanwhile, make the garnish. Half-fill a saucepan with oil and heat to 180–190°C/350–375°F, or until a cube of bread browns in 30 seconds. Add the shredded leek and deep-fry for 1 minute, or until browned and crisp, taking care because it contains water. Drain the shredded leek thoroughly on kitchen paper and reserve.

4 Reserve a few pieces of potato, leek and bacon. Transfer the rest of the soup, in batches, to a food processor or blender and process each batch for 30 seconds. Return the soup to a clean saucepan and heat through.

5 Stir in the reserved vegetables, bacon and chopped parsley, then season to taste with salt and pepper. Pour into warmed soup bowls and garnish with the fried leeks.

VARIATION

For a lighter soup, omit the cream and stir yogurt or crème fraîche into the soup at the end of the cooking time.

wild mushroom soup

serves four

25 g/1 oz dried porcini mushrooms

350 ml/12 fl oz boiling water

125 g/4½ oz fresh porcini
    mushrooms

2 tsp olive oil

1 celery stick, chopped

1 carrot, chopped

1 onion, chopped

3 garlic cloves, crushed

1.2 litres/2 pints vegetable stock
    or water

leaves from 2 fresh thyme sprigs

salt and pepper

1 tbsp butter

3 tbsp dry or medium sherry

2–3 tbsp soured cream

chopped fresh parsley, to garnish

NUTRITION

Calories 130		Sugars 5g
Protein 3g		Fat 9g
Carbohydrate 6g		Saturates 5g

1 Place the dried mushrooms in a bowl and pour the boiling water over them. Leave to soak for 10–15 minutes.

2 Brush or wash the fresh mushrooms. Trim and reserve the stems. Slice any large mushroom caps.

3 Heat the oil in a large saucepan. Add the celery, carrot, onion and mushroom stems and cook, stirring frequently, for 8 minutes, or until the onion begins to colour. Stir in the garlic and continue cooking for 1 minute.

4 Add the stock, thyme leaves and a pinch of salt. Using a slotted spoon, transfer the soaked dried mushrooms to the saucepan. Sieve the soaking liquid through a muslin-lined sieve into the saucepan. Bring to the boil, reduce the heat, partially cover and simmer gently for 30–40 minutes, or until the carrots are tender.

5 Remove the saucepan from the heat and leave to cool slightly, then transfer the soup solids with enough of the cooking liquid to moisten to a food processor or blender and process until smooth. Return the soup to the saucepan, combine with the remaining cooking liquid, cover and simmer gently.

6 Meanwhile, melt the butter in a frying pan. Add the fresh mushroom caps and season to taste with salt and pepper. Cook, stirring occasionally, for 8 minutes, or until they begin to colour, stirring more frequently as the liquid evaporates. When the frying pan becomes dry, add the sherry and cook briefly.

7 Add the mushrooms and sherry to the soup. Taste and adjust the seasoning, if necessary. Ladle into warmed soup bowls, place a spoonful of soured cream in each and garnish with parsley. Serve immediately.

chicken & sweetcorn soup

serves four

2 tsp sunflower oil

15 g/½ oz butter or margarine

1 small onion, finely chopped

1 chicken leg quarter or
    2–3 drumsticks

1 tbsp plain flour

600 ml/1 pint chicken stock

½ small red, yellow or orange
    pepper, deseeded and
    finely chopped

2 large tomatoes, peeled
    and chopped

2 tsp tomato purée

200 g/7 oz canned sweetcorn
    kernels, drained

generous pinch of dried oregano

¼ tsp ground coriander

salt and pepper

chopped fresh parsley, to garnish

NUTRITION

Calories	200	Sugars	6g
Protein	10g	Fat	12g
Carbohydrate	13g	Saturates	5g

1 Heat the oil and butter in a saucepan. Add the onion and fry until beginning to soften. Cut the chicken quarter, if using, into 2 pieces. Add the chicken and fry until golden brown.

2 Add the flour and cook for 1–2 minutes. Add the stock, bring to the boil and simmer for 5 minutes.

3 Add the pepper, tomatoes, tomato purée, sweetcorn, oregano, coriander and salt and pepper to taste. Cover and leave to simmer gently for 20 minutes, or until the chicken is very tender.

4 Remove the chicken from the soup, strip off the flesh and chop finely. Return the chopped meat to the soup.

5 Taste and adjust the seasoning if necessary and simmer for a further 2–3 minutes before sprinkling with parsley and serving very hot.

provençal fish soup

serves four–six

1 tbsp olive oil

2 onions, finely chopped

1 small leek, thinly sliced

1 small carrot, finely chopped

1 celery stick, finely chopped

1 small fennel bulb, finely chopped
    (optional)

3 garlic cloves, finely chopped

225 ml/8 fl oz dry white wine

400 g/14 oz canned tomatoes

1 bay leaf

pinch of fennel seeds

2 strips of orange rind

¼ tsp saffron threads

1.2 litres/2 pints water

350 g/12 oz white fish
    fillets, skinned

salt and pepper

croûtons, to serve (optional)

NUTRITION

Calories 122	Sugars 6g
Protein 12g	Fat 3g
Carbohydrate 7g	Saturates 0g

1 Heat the oil in a large saucepan. Add the onions and cook, stirring occasionally, for 5 minutes, or until softened. Add the leek, carrot, celery, fennel, if using, and garlic and continue cooking for 4–5 minutes, until the leek is wilted.

2 Add the wine and simmer for 1 minute. Add the tomatoes, bay leaf, fennel seeds, orange rind, saffron and water. Bring just to the boil, reduce the heat, cover and simmer gently, stirring occasionally, for 30 minutes.

3 Add the fish and cook for a further 20–30 minutes, or until it flakes easily. Remove and discard the bay leaf and orange rind.

4 Remove the saucepan from the heat and leave to cool slightly, then transfer to a food processor or blender and process to a smooth purée, working in batches if necessary. (If using a food processor, sieve the cooking liquid and reserve. Process the soup solids with enough cooking liquid to moisten them, then combine with the remaining liquid.)

5 Return the soup to the saucepan. Season to taste with salt and pepper, if necessary, then simmer for 5–10 minutes, or until heated through. Ladle the soup into warmed bowls and sprinkle with croûtons, if using. Serve.

beef broth

serves four

200 g/7 oz celeriac, finely diced

2 large carrots, finely diced

2 tsp chopped fresh marjoram

2 tsp chopped fresh parsley

2 plum tomatoes, peeled, deseeded
and diced

salt and pepper

BEEF STOCK

550 g/1 lb 4 oz boneless beef shin
or stewing steak, cut into
large cubes

750 g/1 lb 10 oz veal, beef or
pork bones

2 onions, quartered

2.5 litres/4½ pints water

4 garlic cloves, sliced

2 carrots, sliced

1 large leek, sliced

1 celery stick, cut into 5-cm/
2-inch pieces

1 bay leaf

4–5 fresh thyme sprigs or ¼ tsp
dried thyme

salt

NUTRITION

Calories 21	Sugars 3g
Protein 1g	Fat 1g
Carbohydrate 4g	Saturates 0g

1 Preheat the oven to 190°C/
375°F/Gas Mark 5. To make the
stock, trim the fat from the beef and
place the beef and fat in a large
roasting tin with the bones and onions.
Roast in the oven for 30–40 minutes,
or until browned, turning once or
twice. Transfer to a large flameproof
casserole and drain off the beef fat.

2 Add the water (it should cover
by at least 5 cm/2 inches) and
bring to the boil. Skim off any foam,
reduce the heat and add the garlic,
carrots, leek, celery, bay leaf, thyme
and a pinch of salt. Simmer for
4 hours, skimming occasionally. If the
ingredients emerge from the liquid, top
up with water. Sieve the stock through
a muslin-lined sieve into a container
and remove as much fat as possible.
Use the meat in another recipe and
discard the bones and vegetables.

3 Gently boil the stock until reduced
to 1.5 litres/2¾ pints. Taste and
adjust the seasoning if necessary.

4 Bring a saucepan of salted water
to the boil. Add the celeriac and
carrots, then reduce the heat, cover
and simmer for 15 minutes, or until
tender. Drain. Add the herbs to the
beef stock. Divide the vegetables and
tomatoes between warmed soup
bowls, ladle over the stock and serve.

aïoli

serves four

4 large garlic cloves, or to taste (see
   Cook's Tip, below)
sea salt and pepper
2 large egg yolks
300 ml/10 fl oz extra virgin olive oil
1–2 tbsp lemon juice
1 tbsp fresh white breadcrumbs
TO SERVE
selection of raw vegetables, such as
   sliced red peppers, courgette
   slices, whole spring onions and
   tomato wedges
selection of blanched and cooled
   vegetables, such as baby
   artichoke hearts, cauliflower or
   broccoli florets, or French beans

NUTRITION	
Calories 239	Sugars 0g
Protein 1g	Fat 26g
Carbohydrate 1g	Saturates 4g

1 Finely chop the garlic on a chopping board. Add a pinch of sea salt to the garlic and use the tip and broad side of a knife to work the garlic and salt into a smooth paste.

2 Transfer the garlic paste to a blender or food processor. Add the egg yolks and process until well blended, scraping down the side of the bowl with a rubber spatula, if necessary.

3 With the motor running, slowly pour in the oil in a steady stream through the feeder tube, processing until a thick mayonnaise forms.

4 Add 1 tablespoon of the lemon juice and all the breadcrumbs and process again. Taste and add more lemon juice if necessary. Season to taste with sea salt and pepper.

COOK'S TIP

The amount of garlic in a traditional Provençal aïoli is a matter of personal taste. Local cooks use 2 cloves per person as a rule of thumb, but this version is slightly milder, although still bursting with flavour.

5 Place the aïoli in a bowl, cover and leave to chill until ready to serve. To serve, place the bowl of aïoli on a large platter and surround with a selection of raw and lightly blanched vegetables.

tsatziki

serves twelve

2 large cucumbers

600 ml/1 pint thick natural yogurt

3 garlic cloves, crushed

1 tbsp finely chopped fresh dill

1 tbsp extra virgin olive oil

salt and pepper

TO GARNISH

1 tbsp sesame seeds

cayenne pepper

fresh dill sprigs (optional)

NUTRITION

Calories 75	Sugars 2g
Protein 4g	Fat 6g
Carbohydrate 2g	Saturates 3g

1 Using the coarse side of a grater, grate the cucumbers into a bowl lined with an absorbent, perforated kitchen cloth. Pull up the corners of the cloth to make a tight bundle and squeeze very hard to extract all the moisture (see Cook's Tip).

2 Place the cucumber in another bowl and stir in the yogurt, garlic, dill and oil. Season to taste with salt and pepper. Cover with clingfilm and leave to chill for at least 3 hours to allow the flavours to blend.

3 When ready to serve, remove the dip from the refrigerator and stir. Taste and adjust the seasoning if necessary.

4 Place the sesame seeds in a small, ungreased frying pan and dry-fry them over a medium heat until they turn golden and begin to give off their aroma. Immediately pour them out of the frying pan onto the tsatziki – they will sizzle.

5 Sprinkle some cayenne onto a plate. Lightly dip the tip of a dry pastry brush into the cayenne, then tap a light sprinkling of cayenne over the tsatziki. Garnish with fresh dill sprigs, if using. Ungarnished tsatziki will keep for up to 3 days in the refrigerator.

COOK'S TIP

It is essential to squeeze all the moisture out of the cucumbers in Step 1, or the dip will be unpleasantly watery and will separate.

authentic guacamole

serves four

1 ripe tomato

2 limes

2–3 ripe, small-to-medium
   avocados, or 1–2 large ones

¼–½ onion, finely chopped

pinch of ground cumin

pinch of mild chilli powder

½–1 fresh green chilli, such as
   jalapeño or serrano, deseeded
   and finely chopped

1 tbsp finely chopped fresh
   coriander leaves, plus extra
   to garnish

salt (optional)

tortilla chips or vegetable sticks,
   to serve (optional)

NUTRITION

Calories 212	Sugars 1g
Protein 2g	Fat 21g
Carbohydrate 3g	Saturates 4g

1 Place the tomato in a heatproof bowl, cover with boiling water and leave to stand for 30 seconds. Drain and plunge into cold water. Peel off the skin. Cut the tomato in half, deseed and chop the flesh.

2 Squeeze the juice from the limes into a small bowl. Cut 1 avocado in half around the stone. Twist the 2 halves apart in opposite directions, then remove the stone with a knife. Peel off the skin, dice the flesh and toss in the lime juice to prevent the flesh discolouring. Repeat with the remaining avocados. Mash the avocado flesh coarsely with a fork.

3 Add the onion, tomato, cumin, chilli powder, fresh chilli and finely chopped coriander to the avocados. If using as a dip for tortilla chips, do not add salt. If using as a dip for vegetable sticks, add salt to taste.

4 To serve the guacamole, transfer to a serving dish, garnish with finely chopped coriander and serve with tortilla chips or vegetable sticks.

VARIATION

Try spooning guacamole into soups, especially chicken or seafood. Spoon guacamole over refried beans and melted cheese, then eat it with a salsa of your choice.

hummus

serves eight

200 g/7 oz dried chickpeas

2 large garlic cloves

7 tbsp extra virgin olive oil, plus
  extra for drizzling

2½ tbsp tahini

1 tbsp lemon juice

salt and pepper

paprika

fresh coriander, to garnish

vegetable crudités, to serve

NUTRITION

Calories 204	Sugars 1g
Protein 7g	Fat 14g
Carbohydrate 13g	Saturates 2g

1 Place the chickpeas in a bowl. Pour in at least twice their volume of water and soak for 12 hours, or until they double in size.

2 Drain the chickpeas. Place them in a large flameproof casserole or saucepan and add twice their volume of water. Bring to the boil and boil vigorously for 10 minutes, skimming the surface.

3 Reduce the heat and leave to simmer, skimming the surface occasionally, for 1–2 hours, or until the chickpeas are tender.

4 Meanwhile, cut the garlic in half, remove and discard the green or white cores and roughly chop the cloves. Reserve.

5 Drain the chickpeas, reserving 4 tablespoons of the cooking liquid. Put the olive oil, garlic, tahini and lemon juice in a food processor and process to a smooth paste.

6 Add the chickpeas and pulse until they are finely ground, but the hummus is still lightly textured. Add a little of the reserved cooking liquid if the mixture is too thick. Season to taste with salt and pepper.

7 Scrape the hummus into a bowl, cover and chill in the refrigerator until ready to serve. Drizzle with some oil, sprinkle a little paprika over, garnish with fresh coriander and serve with crudités.

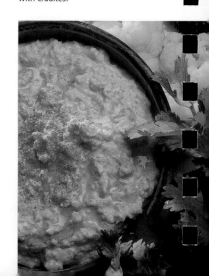

parsley, chicken & ham pâté

serves four

225 g/8 oz skinless, boneless lean
chicken, cooked

100 g/3½ oz lean ham

small bunch of fresh parsley

1 tsp grated lime rind, plus extra
to garnish

2 tbsp lime juice

1 garlic clove, peeled

125 ml/4 fl oz low-fat natural
fromage frais

salt and pepper

TO SERVE

lime wedges

crispbread or Melba toast

NUTRITION

Calories 119	Sugars 2g
Protein 20g	Fat 3g
Carbohydrate 2g	Saturates 1g

1 Roughly dice the chicken. Trim
off and discard any fat from the
ham and dice the meat. Place the
chicken and ham in a food processor.

2 Add the parsley, lime rind and
juice and garlic, and process until
finely minced. Alternatively, finely chop
the chicken, ham, parsley and garlic
and place in a bowl. Gently stir in the
lime rind and juice.

COOK'S TIP

Most types of crispbread
contain around 6 g of
carbohydrate per slice.

3 Transfer the mixture to a bowl
and stir in the fromage frais.
Season to taste with salt and pepper,
cover with clingfilm and chill in the
refrigerator for 30 minutes.

4 Spoon the pâté into individual
serving dishes and garnish with
extra grated lime rind. Serve the pâté
with lime wedges and crispbread.

fat horses

serves four

2 tbsp creamed coconut

115 g/4 oz lean pork

115 g/4 oz skinless, boneless
    chicken breast

115 g/4 oz canned crabmeat,
    drained

2 eggs

2 garlic cloves, crushed

4 spring onions, chopped

1 tbsp Thai fish sauce

1 tbsp chopped fresh coriander
    leaves and stems

1 tbsp dark muscovado sugar

salt and pepper

butter, for greasing

TO GARNISH

finely sliced mooli or turnip

fresh chive lengths

fresh chilli flowers (see page 154)

fresh coriander sprigs

NUTRITION

Calories 195	Sugars 1g
Protein 23g	Fat 11g
Carbohydrate 1g	Saturates 6g

1 Mix the coconut with
3 tablespoons hot water. Stir to
dissolve the coconut.

2 Place the pork, chicken and
crabmeat in a food processor
or blender and process briefly for
10–15 seconds, or until minced.
Alternatively, chop them finely by
hand and place in a large bowl.

3 Add the coconut mixture to the
food processor or blender with
the eggs, garlic, spring onions, fish
sauce, coriander and sugar. Season to
taste with salt and pepper and process
for a few more seconds. Alternatively,
mix these ingredients into the chopped
pork, chicken and crabmeat.

4 Grease 6 ramekin dishes with a
little butter. Spoon in the minced
mixture, smoothing the surface. Place
them in a steamer, then set the steamer
over a saucepan of gently simmering
water. Cook for 30 minutes, or until set.

5 Lift out the dishes and leave to
cool for a few minutes. Run a
knife around the edge of each dish,
then invert onto warmed plates. Serve
immediately, garnished with finely
sliced mooli, fresh chives, a red chilli
flower and fresh coriander sprigs.

aubergine dip

Serves six–eight

2 large aubergines

1 tomato

1 garlic clove, chopped

4 tbsp extra virgin olive oil

2 tbsp lemon juice

2 tbsp pine kernels, lightly toasted

salt and pepper

2 spring onions, finely chopped

fresh vegetables, to serve

TO GARNISH

ground cumin

2 tbsp finely chopped fresh
   flat-leaf parsley

NUTRITION	
Calories 90	Sugars 2g
Protein 1g	Fat 8g
Carbohydrate 2g	Saturates 1g

1 Preheat the oven to 230°C/
450°F/Gas Mark 8. Using
a fork or metal skewer, pierce the
aubergines all over. Place them on a
large baking sheet and roast in the
preheated oven for 20–25 minutes,
or until they are very soft.

2 Use a folded tea towel to remove
the aubergines from the baking
sheet and leave to cool.

3 Place the tomato in a heatproof
bowl, pour boiling water over to
cover and leave for 30 seconds. Drain,
then plunge into cold water to prevent
it cooking. Peel the tomato, then cut in
half and scoop out the seeds with a
teaspoon. Finely dice the flesh
and reserve.

4 Cut the cooled aubergines in half
lengthways. Scoop out the flesh
with a spoon and transfer to a food
processor. Add the garlic, oil, lemon
juice and pine kernels and season with
salt and pepper to taste. Process until
smooth. Alternatively, mash by hand.

5 Scrape the mixture into a bowl
and stir in the spring onions and
diced tomato. Cover and leave to chill
for 30 minutes before serving.

6 Garnish the dip with a pinch
of cumin and chopped parsley,
then serve with fresh vegetables.

aubergine rolls

serves four

2 aubergines, thinly sliced
    lengthways
salt and pepper
5 tbsp olive oil, plus extra
    for brushing
1 garlic clove, crushed
4 tbsp pesto
175 g/6 oz mozzarella cheese,
    grated
basil leaves, torn into pieces
fresh basil leaves, to garnish

NUTRITION

Calories 278		Sugars 2g
Protein 4g		Fat 28g
Carbohydrate 2g		Saturates 7g

COOK'S TIP

Most aubergines produced
commercially these days do
not have bitter juices that must
be removed before cooking.
Nevertheless, salting is a good
idea if the aubergines are to be
fried, because it prevents them
absorbing too much oil.

1 Preheat the oven to 180°C/
350°F/Gas Mark 4. Sprinkle the
aubergine slices liberally with salt and
leave for 10–15 minutes to extract the
juices. Turn the slices over and repeat.
Rinse well with cold water and drain
on kitchen paper.

2 Heat the oil in a large frying pan.
Add the garlic and aubergine
slices, a few at a time, and fry the
aubergine lightly on both sides.
Remove with a slotted spoon and drain
on slotted paper.

3 Spread a little pesto onto one side
of each of the aubergine slices.
Top with the grated mozzarella cheese
and sprinkle with the torn basil leaves.
Season with a little salt and pepper.
Roll up the slices and secure them with
wooden cocktail sticks.

4 Arrange the aubergine rolls in a
greased ovenproof baking dish
and bake in the preheated oven for
8–10 minutes.

5 Transfer the aubergine rolls to a
warmed serving plate. Sprinkle
with fresh basil leaves and serve.

soufflé omelette

serves four

175 g/6 oz cherry tomatoes

225 g/8 oz mixed mushrooms, such
   as button, chestnut, shiitake
   and oyster

4 tbsp vegetable stock

small bunch of fresh thyme, tied
   with string

4 eggs

125 ml/4 fl oz water

4 egg whites

4 tsp olive oil

25 g/1 oz rocket leaves

fresh thyme sprigs, to garnish

NUTRITION

Calories 146	Sugars 2g
Protein 10g	Fat 11g
Carbohydrate 2g	Saturates 2g

1 Halve the tomatoes and place them in a saucepan. Wipe the mushrooms with kitchen paper, trim if necessary and slice if large. Place the mushrooms in the saucepan with the tomatoes.

2 Add the stock and the bunch of thyme to the pan. Bring to the boil, cover and simmer for 5–6 minutes until tender. Drain, remove the thyme and discard. Keep the mixture warm.

3 Meanwhile, separate the eggs and whisk the egg yolks with the water until frothy. Whisk the 8 egg whites in a clean, grease-free bowl until stiff and dry.

4 Spoon the egg yolk mixture into the egg whites and, using a metal spoon, fold together until well mixed. Take care not to knock out too much of the air.

5 Preheat the grill to medium. For each omelette, brush a small omelette pan with 1 teaspoon of the oil and heat until hot. Pour in a quarter of the egg mixture and cook for 4–5 minutes, or until the mixture has set.

6 Finish cooking the omelette under the hot grill for 2–3 minutes.

7 Transfer the omelette to a warmed serving plate. Fill the omelette with a few rocket leaves and a quarter of the mushroom and tomato mixture. Flip over the top of the omelette, garnish with fresh thyme sprigs and serve.

spinach cheese moulds

serves four

100 g/3½ oz fresh spinach leaves
300 g/10½ oz skimmed milk
  soft cheese
2 garlic cloves, crushed
fresh parsley, tarragon and chive
  sprigs, finely chopped
salt and pepper
mixed salad leaves and fresh herbs,
  to serve

NUTRITION

Calories 119	Sugars 2g
Protein 6g	Fat 9g
Carbohydrate 2g	Saturates 6g

1 Trim the stalks from the spinach leaves and rinse the leaves under cold running water. Pack the leaves into a saucepan while they are still wet, cover and cook over a medium heat for 3–4 minutes, or until wilted – they will cook in the steam from the wet leaves (do not overcook). Drain well and pat dry with kitchen paper.

2 Line the bases of 4 small pudding basins or individual ramekin dishes with baking paper. Line the basins with the spinach leaves so that the leaves overhang the edges.

3 Place the cheese in a bowl and add the garlic and herbs. Mix together thoroughly and season to taste with salt and pepper.

4 Spoon the cheese and herb mixture into the basins and pull over the overlapping spinach to cover the cheese, or lay extra leaves to cover the top. Place a greaseproof paper disc on top of each dish and weigh down with a 100 g/3½ oz weight. Leave to chill in the refrigerator for 1 hour.

5 Remove the weights and peel off the paper. Loosen the moulds gently by running a small palette knife around the edges of each dish and turn them out onto individual serving plates. Serve immediately with a mixture of salad leaves and fresh herbs.

figs & parma ham

serves four

40 g/1½ oz rocket leaves

4 fresh figs

4 slices Parma ham

4 tbsp olive oil

1 tbsp fresh orange juice

1 tbsp clear honey

1 small fresh red chilli

1 Tear the rocket leaves into manageable pieces and arrange on 4 individual serving plates.

2 Using a sharp knife, cut each of the figs into quarters and place them on top of the rocket leaves.

COOK'S TIP

Fresh chillies can burn the skin for several hours after chopping, so it is advisable to wear gloves when you are handling any very hot varieties and to wash your hands afterwards.

NUTRITION

Calories 121	Sugars 6g
Protein 1g	Fat 11g
Carbohydrate 6g	Saturates 2g

3 Using a sharp knife, cut the Parma ham into strips and sprinkle over the rocket and figs.

4 Place the oil, orange juice and honey in a screw-top jar. Shake the jar vigorously until the mixture emulsifies and forms a thick dressing. Transfer the dressing to a bowl.

5 Using a sharp knife, dice the chilli. (You can remove the seeds first if you prefer a milder flavour.) Add the diced chilli to the dressing and mix well.

6 Drizzle the dressing over the Parma ham, rocket and figs, tossing to mix well. Serve immediately.

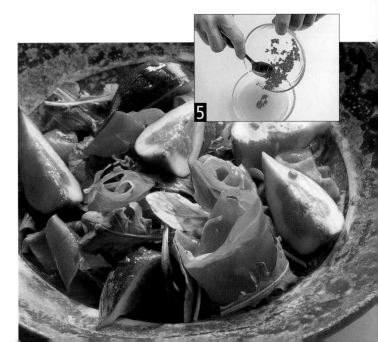

aubergine & rice rolls

serves four

3 aubergines (total weight about
750 g / 1 lb 10 oz)

55 g/2 oz mixed long-grain and
wild rice

4 spring onions, thinly sliced

3 tbsp chopped cashew nuts or
toasted chopped hazelnuts

2 tbsp capers, drained and rinsed

1 garlic clove, crushed

2 tbsp freshly grated
Parmesan cheese

1 egg, beaten

salt and pepper

1 tbsp olive oil, plus extra
for oiling

1 tbsp balsamic vinegar

2 tbsp tomato purée

150 ml/5 fl oz water

150 ml/5 fl oz dry white wine

fresh coriander sprigs, to garnish

NUTRITION

Calories 142	Sugars 3g
Protein 6g	Fat 9g
Carbohydrate 9g	Saturates 3g

1 Preheat the oven to 180°C/
350°F/Gas Mark 4. Cut off the
stem end of each aubergine, then cut
off and discard a strip of skin from
alternate sides of each aubergine.
Cut each aubergine into thin slices to
give a total of 16 slices.

2 Blanch the aubergine slices in
boiling water for 5 minutes, then
drain on kitchen paper.

3 Cook the rice in boiling salted
water for 12 minutes, or until just
tender. Drain and place in a bowl. Add
the spring onions, nuts, capers, garlic,
cheese, egg and salt and pepper to
taste, and stir well.

4 Spread a thin layer of rice mixture
over each slice of aubergine and
roll up, securing with a cocktail stick.
Place the rolls in an oiled flameproof
dish and brush each one with oil.

5 Mix the vinegar, tomato purée
and water together. Pour over the
rolls. Cook in the oven for 40 minutes,
or until tender and most of the liquid
has been absorbed. Transfer to a dish.

6 Add the wine to the pan juices
and heat until the sediment
loosens, then simmer for 2–3 minutes.
Taste and adjust the seasoning if
necessary and sieve the sauce over the
aubergine rolls. Leave until cold, then
chill thoroughly.

7 Garnish the aubergine rolls with
fresh coriander sprigs and serve.

crispy pork & peanut baskets

serves four

2 sheets filo pastry, each about
    42 x 28 cm/16½ x 11 inches
2 tbsp vegetable oil
1 garlic clove, crushed
125 g/4½ oz fresh pork mince
1 tsp Thai red curry paste
2 spring onions, finely chopped
3 tbsp crunchy peanut butter
1 tbsp light soy sauce
1 tbsp chopped fresh coriander
salt and pepper
fresh coriander sprigs, to garnish

COOK'S TIP

When using filo pastry, remember that it dries out very quickly and becomes brittle and difficult to handle. Work quickly and keep any sheets of pastry you're not using covered with clingfilm and a dampened cloth.

NUTRITION

Calories 243	Sugars 1g
Protein 12g	Fat 16g
Carbohydrate 12g	Saturates 3g

1 Preheat the oven to 200°C/ 400°F/Gas Mark 6. Cut each sheet of filo pastry into 24 squares, 7 cm/2¾ inches across, to make a total of 48 squares. Brush each square lightly with oil, and arrange the squares in stacks of 4 in 12 small patty tins, pointing outwards. Press the pastry down into the patty tins.

2 Bake the pastry cases in the preheated oven for 6–8 minutes, or until golden brown.

3 Meanwhile, heat 1 tablespoon of the oil in a preheated wok. Add the garlic and fry for 30 seconds, then stir in the pork and stir-fry over a high heat for 4–5 minutes, or until the meat is golden brown.

4 Add the curry paste and spring onions and continue to stir-fry for a further 1 minute, then stir in the peanut butter, soy sauce and chopped coriander. Season to taste with salt and pepper.

5 Spoon the pork mixture into the filo baskets and serve hot, garnished with coriander sprigs.

crispy golden seafood

serves four

200 g/7 oz prepared squid

200 g/7 oz raw blue tiger prawns, peeled

150 g/5½ oz whitebait

300 ml/10 fl oz oil, for deep-frying

50 g/1¾ oz plain flour

salt and pepper

1 tsp dried basil

Garlic Mayonnaise, to serve

(see Cook's Tip)

COOK'S TIP

To make the Garlic Mayonnaise, crush 2 garlic cloves, stir into 8 tablespoons of mayonnaise and season to taste with salt and pepper and 1 tablespoon of chopped fresh parsley. Cover and chill in the refrigerator until ready to serve.

NUTRITION

Calories 393		Sugars 0.2g	
Protein 27g		Fat 26g	
Carbohydrate 12g		Saturates 3g	

1 Carefully rinse the squid, prawns and whitebait under cold running water, completely removing any accumulated dirt or grit.

2 Using a sharp knife, slice the squid into thick rings, but leave all the tentacles whole.

3 Heat the oil in a large saucepan to 180–190°C/350–375°F, or until a cube of bread browns in 30 seconds.

4 Place the flour in a large bowl and season to taste with salt, pepper and the dried basil.

5 Toss the squid, prawns and whitebait in the seasoned flour until coated thoroughly all over. Carefully shake off any excess flour.

6 Cook the seafood, in batches, in the hot oil for 2–3 minutes, or until crispy and golden all over. Remove each batch of seafood with a slotted spoon and leave to drain thoroughly on kitchen paper.

7 Transfer the deep-fried seafood to 4 large serving plates and serve immediately with the Garlic Mayonnaise (see Cook's Tip).

steamed crab cakes

serves four

1–2 banana leaves

2 garlic cloves, crushed

1 tsp finely chopped lemon grass

½ tsp pepper

2 tbsp chopped fresh coriander

3 tbsp creamed coconut

1 tbsp lime juice

200 g/7 oz cooked crabmeat, flaked

1 tbsp Thai fish sauce

2 egg whites

1 egg yolk, lightly beaten

8 fresh coriander leaves

sunflower oil, for deep-frying

chilli sauce, to serve

NUTRITION

Calories 156		Sugars 1g	
Protein 13g		Fat 11g	
Carbohydrate 2g		Saturates 4g	

1 Line 8 x 100-ml/3½-fl oz ramekin dishes or foil containers with the banana leaves, cutting them to shape.

2 Mix the garlic, lemon grass, pepper and coriander together. Mash the creamed coconut with the lime juice until smooth. Stir it into the other ingredients with the crabmeat and fish sauce.

3 Whisk the egg whites in a clean, dry bowl until stiff, then lightly and evenly fold them into the crab mixture.

4 Spoon the mixture into the prepared ramekin dishes and press down lightly. Brush the tops with egg yolk and top each with a coriander leaf.

5 Place in a steamer half-filled with boiling water, then cover with a close-fitting lid and steam for 15 minutes, or until firm to the touch. Pour off the excess liquid and remove from the ramekin dishes.

6 Heat the oil to 180–190°C/ 350–375°F, or until a cube of bread browns in 30 seconds. Add the crab cakes and deep-fry for 1 minute, turning them over once, or until golden brown. Serve hot with chilli sauce.

sardines with pesto

serves four

16 large sardines, scaled and gutted
55 g/2 oz fresh basil leaves
2 garlic cloves, crushed
2 tbsp pine kernels, toasted
55 g/2 oz freshly grated
   Parmesan cheese
150 ml/5 fl oz olive oil
salt and pepper
lemon wedges, to garnish

NUTRITION

Calories 617	Sugars 0g
Protein 27g	Fat 56g
Carbohydrate 1g	Saturates 11g

1 Preheat the grill. Wash the sardines and pat dry with kitchen paper. Arrange them on a grill pan.

2 Place the basil leaves, garlic and pine kernels in a food processor and process until finely chopped. Transfer to a small bowl and stir in the Parmesan and oil. Season to taste with salt and pepper.

3 Spread a little of the pesto over one side of the sardines and place under the hot grill for 3 minutes. Turn the fish, spread with more pesto and grill for a further 3 minutes, or until the fish are cooked through.

4 Serve the sardines immediately with extra pesto and garnished with lemon wedges.

VARIATION
This treatment will also work well with other small oily fish such as herrings and sprats.

wild rice blinis

serves four–six

butter or vegetable oil, for frying

4 spring onions, thinly sliced
   diagonally

115 g/4 oz smoked salmon,
   thinly sliced into strips
   or shredded

125 ml /4 fl oz soured cream

snipped fresh chives, to sprinkle

BLINIS

75 ml/2½ fl oz lukewarm water

1½ tsp dried yeast

55 g/2 oz plain flour

70 g/2½ oz buckwheat flour

2 tbsp sugar

½ tsp salt

225 ml/8 fl oz milk

2 eggs, separated

2 tbsp butter, melted

55 g/2 oz cooked wild rice

TO GARNISH

orange twist

fresh mint sprig

NUTRITION

Calories 37	Sugars 1g
Protein 1g	Fat 2g
Carbohydrate 4g	Saturates 1g

1 To make the blinis, pour the water into a small bowl and sprinkle the yeast over it. Leave to stand until the yeast has dissolved and the mixture is beginning to froth.

2 Sift the flours into a bowl and stir in the sugar and salt. Make a well in the centre. Warm 175 ml/6 fl oz of the milk and add to the well with the yeast mixture. Gradually whisk the flour into the liquid to form a smooth batter. Cover and leave in a warm place until light and bubbly.

3 Beat the remaining milk with the egg yolks and the melted butter and then beat into the batter.

4 Using an electric mixer, whisk the egg whites until soft peaks form. Fold a spoonful into the batter, then fold in the remaining egg whites and the rice alternately. Do not overmix.

5 Heat just enough butter in a large frying pan to coat lightly. Drop tablespoonfuls of the batter into the frying pan and cook for 1–2 minutes, or until tiny bubbles form on the surface. Turn and cook for 30 seconds. Remove and keep warm in a low oven while cooking the remaining batter. Add a little more butter if necessary.

6 Top with the spring onions, smoked salmon, soured cream and a sprinkling of snipped chives. Garnish with an orange twist and fresh mint sprig and serve.

57

bang-bang chicken

serves four

1 litre/1¾ pints water

2 chicken quarters

1 cucumber, cut into
    matchstick shreds

SAUCE

2 tbsp light soy sauce

1 tsp sugar

1 tbsp finely chopped spring onions,
    plus extra to garnish

1 tsp red chilli oil

¼ tsp pepper

1 tsp white sesame seeds,
    plus extra to garnish

2 tbsp peanut butter, creamed with
    a little sesame oil

NUTRITION	
Calories 82	Sugars 1g
Protein 13g	Fat 3g
Carbohydrate 2g	Saturates 1g

1 Bring the water to a rolling boil in a large saucepan. Add the chicken pieces, reduce the heat, cover and cook for 30–35 minutes.

2 Remove the chicken from the saucepan and immerse in a bowl of cold water for at least 1 hour, to cool it ready for shredding.

3 Remove the chicken pieces, drain and dry on kitchen paper. Take the meat off the bone.

4 Pound the chicken with a rolling pin on a flat surface, then tear the meat into shreds with 2 forks. Mix the chicken with the shredded cucumber and arrange in a serving dish.

5 To serve, mix all the sauce ingredients together until thoroughly combined and pour over the chicken and cucumber in the serving dish. Sprinkle some sesame seeds and chopped spring onions over the sauce and serve.

COOK'S TIP

Take the time to tear the chicken meat into similar-sized shreds, to make an elegant-looking dish. You can do this quite efficiently with 2 forks, although Chinese cooks would do it with their fingers.

turkey & vegetable loaf

serves six

1 onion, finely chopped

1 garlic clove, crushed

900 g/2 lb lean fresh turkey mince

1 tbsp chopped fresh parsley

1 tbsp snipped fresh chives

1 tbsp chopped fresh tarragon

salt and pepper

1 egg white, lightly beaten

2 courgettes, 1 medium and 1 large

2 tomatoes

tomato and herb sauce, to serve
  (optional)

NUTRITION

Calories 165	Sugars 1g
Protein 36g	Fat 2g
Carbohydrate 1g	Saturates 0.5g

COOK'S TIP

To test if the loaf is cooked, insert a skewer into the centre – the juices should run clear. The loaf will also shrink away from the sides of the tin.

1 Preheat the oven to 190°C/375°F/ Gas Mark 5. Line a non-stick loaf tin with baking paper. Place the onion, garlic and turkey in a bowl, add the herbs and season to taste with salt and pepper. Mix together with your hands, then add the egg white to bind the mixture together.

2 Press half of the turkey mixture into the base of the tin. Thinly slice the medium courgette and the tomatoes and arrange the slices over the meat. Top with the rest of the turkey mixture and press down firmly. Cover with a layer of foil and place in a roasting tin. Pour in enough boiling water to come halfway up the sides of the loaf tin. Bake in the oven for 1–1¼ hours, removing the foil for the last 20 minutes of cooking.

3 Cut the large courgette lengthways into thin slices with a vegetable peeler. Bring a saucepan of water to the boil and blanch the courgette for 1–2 minutes, or until just tender. Drain and keep warm.

4 Remove the loaf from the tin and transfer to a warmed serving platter. Drape the courgette ribbons over the turkey loaf and serve with a tomato and herb sauce, if you like.

asian pork balls in broth

serves six

2 litres/3½ pints chicken stock
85 g/3 oz shiitake mushrooms,
    thinly sliced
175 g/6 oz pak choi or other
    Chinese greens, sliced into
    thin ribbons
6 spring onions, finely sliced
salt and pepper
PORK BALLS
225 g/8 oz lean fresh pork mince
25 g/1 oz fresh spinach leaves,
    finely chopped
2 spring onions, finely chopped
1 garlic clove, very finely chopped
pinch of Chinese five-spice powder
1 tsp soy sauce

NUTRITION

Calories 67	Sugars 1g
Protein 9g	Fat 2g
Carbohydrate 3g	Saturates 1g

1 To make the pork balls, place the pork, spinach, spring onions and garlic in a bowl. Add the five-spice powder and soy sauce and mix until thoroughly combined.

2 Shape the pork mixture into 24 balls. Place them in a single layer in a steamer that will fit over the top of a large saucepan.

3 Bring the stock just to the boil in a saucepan that will accommodate the steamer. Reduce the heat so that the liquid just bubbles gently. Add the mushrooms to the stock and place the steamer, covered, on top of the saucepan. Steam for 10 minutes. Remove the steamer and leave to stand on a plate.

4 Add the pak choi and spring onions to the saucepan and cook gently in the stock for 3–4 minutes, or until the leaves are wilted. Season the broth to taste with salt and pepper.

5 Divide the pork balls evenly between 6 warmed serving bowls and ladle the soup over them. Serve immediately.

spare ribs

serves four

900 g/2 lb pork spare ribs

2 tbsp dark soy sauce

3 tbsp hoisin sauce

1 tbsp rice wine or dry sherry

pinch of Chinese five-spice powder

2 tsp dark brown sugar

¼ tsp chilli sauce

2 garlic cloves, crushed

fresh coriander sprigs, to garnish
  (optional)

NUTRITION

Calories 436	Sugars 3g
Protein 21g	Fat 37g
Carbohydrate 3g	Saturates 14g

1 Cut the spare ribs into separate pieces if they are joined together. If desired, you can chop them into 5-cm/2-inch lengths, using a cleaver.

2 Mix the soy sauce, hoisin sauce, rice wine, five-spice powder, brown sugar, chilli sauce and garlic together in a large bowl.

3 Place the ribs in a shallow dish and pour the mixture over them, turning to coat the ribs thoroughly. Cover with clingfilm and leave to marinate in the refrigerator, turning the ribs occasionally, for at least 1 hour.

4 Preheat the oven to 180°C/350°F/ Gas Mark 4. Remove the ribs from the marinade and arrange them in a single layer on a wire rack placed over a roasting tin half-filled with warm water. Using a pastry brush, coat the ribs with the marinade, reserving the remaining marinade.

5 Cook the ribs in the preheated oven for 30 minutes. Remove the roasting tin from the oven and turn the ribs over. Brush with the remaining marinade and return to the oven for a further 30 minutes, or until cooked through. Add more hot water to the roasting tin during cooking, if required. Do not allow it to dry out because the water steams the ribs and aids in their cooking.

6 Transfer the ribs to a warmed serving dish, garnish with fresh coriander sprigs, if using, and serve immediately.

Snacks & Side Dishes

Vegetables in their wealth of different forms are rich in essential nutrients, and the more varieties you eat, the greater the range of these health-promoting vitamins and minerals you can benefit from. The following recipes take the pick of the crop and, using a range of cooking methods and seasonings, turn them into truly exciting and tempting dishes – perfect for serving with grilled or barbecued meat, poultry or fish, or to enjoy on their own as a filler at any time of day. Try the speedy Pak Choi with Crabmeat (see page 70) or opt for the slower-paced Braised Fennel (see page 78).

Salads are another low-carbohydrate mainstay, and offer a feast of fresh flavour and colour – like the Grapefruit & Cheese Salad (see page 96), with pink grapefruit and avocado, or the Smoked Trout & Apple Salad (see page 92), with chives and chive flowers.

sesame seed chutney

serves four

8 tbsp sesame seeds

2 tbsp water

½ bunch of fresh coriander

3 fresh green chillies, deseeded
    and chopped

1 tsp salt

2 tsp lemon juice

chopped fresh red chilli, to garnish

NUTRITION

Calories 120	Sugars 0g
Protein 4g	Fat 12g
Carbohydrate 0.2g	Saturates 2g

COOK'S TIP

Dry roasting brings out the flavour of spices and takes just a few minutes. You will be able to tell when the spices are ready because of the wonderful fragrance that develops. Stir the spices constantly to ensure that they do not burn.

1 Place the sesame seeds in a large heavy-based saucepan and dry roast them, stirring constantly. Remove from the heat and leave to cool.

2 Once cooled, place the sesame seeds in a mortar or food processor and grind well to form a fine powder.

3 Add the water to the ground sesame seeds and mix thoroughly to form a smooth paste.

4 Finely chop the coriander. Add the chillies and coriander to the sesame seed paste and grind again.

5 Add the salt and the lemon juice to the mixture and grind once again.

6 Transfer the mixture to a serving dish. Garnish with chopped red chilli and serve.

okra bhaji

serves four

1 tbsp sunflower oil

1 tsp black mustard seeds

1 tsp cumin seeds

1 tsp ground coriander

½ tsp ground turmeric

1 fresh green chilli, deseeded and
    finely chopped

1 red onion, finely sliced

2 garlic cloves, crushed

1 orange pepper, deseeded and
    thinly sliced

500 g/1 lb 2 oz okra, blanched

250 ml/9 fl oz vegetable juice

salt

150 ml/5 fl oz single cream

1 tbsp lemon juice

NUTRITION

Calories 173	Sugars 11g
Protein 6g	Fat 11g
Carbohydrate 13g	Saturates 5g

1 Heat the oil in a preheated wok or large heavy-based frying pan. Add the mustard seeds and cover the wok until they begin to pop.

2 Stir in the cumin seeds, ground coriander, turmeric and chilli. Stir constantly for 1 minute, or until the spices give off their aroma.

3 Add the onion, garlic and pepper, and cook, stirring frequently, for 5 minutes, or until soft.

4 Add the blanched okra to the wok and stir well.

5 Pour in the vegetable juice, bring to the boil and cook over a high heat, stirring occasionally, for 5 minutes.

6 When most of the liquid has evaporated, taste and adjust the seasoning, adding salt if necessary.

7 Add the cream, return to the boil and continue to cook the mixture over a high heat for 12 minutes, or until it is almost dry.

8 Sprinkle the lemon juice over the okra bhaji. Transfer to a warmed serving dish and serve immediately.

vegetables à la grecque

serves four–six

250 g/9 oz small pickling onions

250 g/9 oz mushrooms

250 g/9 oz courgettes

450 ml/16 fl oz water

5 tbsp olive oil

2 tbsp lemon juice

2 strips lemon rind

2 large garlic cloves, thinly sliced

½ Spanish onion, finely chopped

1 bay leaf

15 black peppercorns,
   lightly crushed

10 coriander seeds, lightly crushed

pinch of dried oregano

finely chopped fresh flat-leaf parsley
   or coriander, to garnish

NUTRITION

Calories 67		Sugars 4g
Protein 2g		Fat 4g
Carbohydrate 6g		Saturates 1g

1 Place the pickling onions in a heatproof bowl and cover with boiling water. Leave for 2 minutes, then drain. Peel and reserve.

2 Trim the mushroom stems. Cut the mushrooms into halves or quarters, or leave whole if small. Cut thin strips of peel from the courgettes for a decorative finish, then cut into 5-mm/¼-inch slices. Reserve the mushrooms and courgettes.

3 Place the water, oil, lemon juice and rind, garlic, Spanish onion, bay leaf, peppercorns, coriander seeds and oregano in a saucepan over a high heat and bring to the boil. Reduce the heat and simmer for 15 minutes.

4 Add the small onions and continue to simmer for 5 minutes. Add the mushrooms and courgettes and simmer for a further 2 minutes.

5 Using a slotted spoon, transfer all the vegetables to a large heatproof dish.

6 Return the liquid to the boil and boil until reduced to 6 tablespoons. Pour the liquid over the vegetables and leave to cool completely.

7 Cover with clingfilm and leave to chill for at least 12 hours.

8 To serve, place the vegetables and cooking liquid in a serving dish and sprinkle the fresh herbs over them.

pak choi with crabmeat

serves four

2 heads pak choi, about 250 g/
9 oz total weight

2 tbsp vegetable oil

1 garlic clove, thinly sliced

2 tbsp oyster sauce

100 g/3½ oz cherry tomatoes,
halved

175 g/6 oz canned white
crabmeat, drained

salt and pepper

VARIATION

If pak choi is not available,
Chinese leaves make a good
alternative for this dish.

1 Trim the pak choi and cut into
2.5-cm/1-inch thick slices.

2 Heat the oil in a large frying pan
or wok. Add the garlic and stir-fry
over a high heat for 1 minute.

3 Add the pak choi and stir-fry for
2–3 minutes, or until the leaves
wilt but the stalks are still crisp.

4 Add the oyster sauce and cherry
tomatoes and stir-fry for a further
1 minute.

5 Add the crabmeat and season to
taste with salt and pepper. Stir to
heat thoroughly and break up the
distribution of crabmeat before serving.

NUTRITION	
Calories 101	Sugars 2g
Protein 9g	Fat 6g
Carbohydrate 3g	Saturates 1g

stir-fried ginger mushrooms

serves four

2 tbsp vegetable oil

3 garlic cloves, crushed

1 tbsp Thai red curry paste

½ tsp ground turmeric

425 g/15 oz canned straw
   mushrooms, drained and halved

2-cm/¾-inch piece fresh root ginger,
   finely shredded

100 ml/3½ fl oz coconut milk

40 g/1½ oz dried shiitake
   mushrooms, soaked, drained
   and sliced

1 tbsp lemon juice

1 tbsp light soy sauce

2 tsp sugar

½ tsp salt

8 cherry tomatoes, halved

200 g/7 oz firm tofu
   (drained weight), diced

fresh coriander leaves, to garnish

1 Heat the oil in a frying pan. Add the garlic and stir-fry for 1 minute. Stir in the curry paste and turmeric and cook for a further 30 seconds.

2 Stir in the straw mushrooms and ginger and stir-fry for 2 minutes. Stir in the coconut milk and bring to the boil.

3 Stir in the dried shiitake mushrooms, lemon juice, soy sauce, sugar and salt and heat thoroughly. Add the tomatoes and tofu and toss gently to heat through.

4 Sprinkle the coriander leaves over the mixture and serve immediately.

NUTRITION

Calories 174	Sugars 7g
Protein 8g	Fat 9g
Carbohydrate 15g	Saturates 1g

brindil bhaji

serves four

500 g/1 lb 2 oz aubergines, sliced

2 tbsp ghee or vegetable oil

1 onion, thinly sliced

2 garlic cloves, sliced

2.5-cm/1-inch piece fresh root
    ginger, grated

½ tsp ground turmeric

1 dried red chilli, finely chopped

½ tsp salt

400 g/14 oz canned tomatoes

1 tsp garam masala

fresh coriander sprigs, to garnish

NUTRITION

Calories 117	Sugars 8g
Protein 3g	Fat 8g
Carbohydrate 9g	Saturates 5g

VARIATION

Other vegetables can be used
instead of the aubergines. Try
courgettes, potatoes or peppers,
or any combination of these
vegetables, using the
same sauce.

1 Cut the aubergine slices into
finger-width strips.

2 Heat the ghee in a heavy-based
saucepan. Add the onion and
cook over a medium heat, stirring
constantly, for 7–8 minutes, or until
very soft and just beginning to colour.

3 Add the garlic and aubergine
strips, increase the heat and cook,
stirring constantly, for 2 minutes. Stir
in the ginger, turmeric, chilli, salt and
tomatoes with their can juices. Use
the back of a wooden spoon to break
up the tomatoes. Reduce the heat and
leave to simmer, uncovered, for
15–20 minutes, or until the aubergines
are very soft.

4 Stir in the garam masala and
simmer for a further 4–5 minutes.

5 Transfer the brindil bhaji to a
warmed serving plate, garnish
with fresh coriander sprigs and
serve immediately.

roasted vegetables

serves six

1 small red cabbage

1 fennel bulb

1 orange pepper, cut into 4-cm/
1½-inch dice

1 aubergine, halved and sliced into
1-cm/½-inch pieces

2 courgettes, thickly sliced
diagonally

6 rosemary twigs, about 15 cm/
6 inches long, soaked in
cold water

olive oil, for brushing

salt and pepper

NUTRITION

Calories 16	Sugars 3g
Protein 1g	Fat 0.3g
Carbohydrate 3g	Saturates 0g

1 Preheat the grill or barbecue. Cut the red cabbage through the middle of its stem and heart. Divide each piece into 4, each time including a section of the stem in the slice to hold it together.

2 Prepare the fennel in the same way as the red cabbage.

3 Blanch the red cabbage and fennel in boiling water for 3 minutes, then drain well.

4 With a wooden skewer, carefully pierce a hole through the middle of each piece of vegetable.

VARIATION

Fruit skewers are a deliciously quick and easy dessert. Thread pieces of banana, mango, peach, strawberry, apple and pear onto soaked wooden skewers and cook over the dying embers of a barbecue. Brush with sugar syrup towards the end of cooking.

5 Thread a piece of orange pepper, fennel, red cabbage, aubergine and courgette onto each rosemary twig, gently pushing the rosemary through the skewer holes.

6 Brush liberally with oil and season with plenty of salt and pepper.

7 Cook under the hot grill or over hot coals for 8–10 minutes, turning occasionally. Serve.

tomato sauce

serves four

1 tbsp olive oil

1 small onion, chopped

1 garlic clove, crushed

200 g/7 oz canned chopped
    tomatoes

2 tsp tomato purée

½ tsp sugar

½ tsp dried oregano

1 bay leaf

salt and pepper

NUTRITION	
Calories 41	Sugars 3g
Protein 1g	Fat 3g
Carbohydrate 3g	Saturates 0.4g

1 Heat the oil in a saucepan. Add the onion and garlic and fry for 5 minutes, or until soft but not browned.

2 Add the tomatoes, tomato purée, sugar, oregano, bay leaf and salt and pepper to taste. Stir well.

3 Bring the sauce to the boil, cover and leave to simmer gently for 20 minutes, stirring occasionally, or until you have a thickish sauce.

4 Remove the bay leaf and season to taste with salt and pepper. Leave to cool completely before using. This sauce keeps well in a screw-top jar in the refrigerator for up to 1 week.

roast leeks

serves four

4 leeks

3 tbsp olive oil

2 tsp balsamic vinegar

sea salt and pepper

NUTRITION

Calories 71	Sugars 2g
Protein 2g	Fat 6g
Carbohydrate 3g	Saturates 1g

COOK'S TIP

Use a good quality French or
Italian olive oil for this deliciously
simple yet sophisticated
vegetable accompaniment.

1 Preheat the barbecue. Cut the leeks in half lengthways, making sure that you hold the knife straight, so that the leek is held together by the root. Brush each leek liberally with oil.

2 Cook the leeks over hot coals for 6–7 minutes, turning once.

3 Remove the leeks from the barbecue and brush them lightly with the vinegar.

4 Season to taste with salt and pepper and serve hot or warm.

sweet & sour courgettes

serves four–six

500 g/1 lb 2 oz courgettes

3 tbsp olive oil

1 large garlic clove, finely chopped

3 tbsp white wine vinegar

3 tbsp water

6–8 anchovy fillets, canned
  or salted

3 tbsp pine kernels

3 tbsp raisins

salt and pepper

fresh flat-leaf parsley sprigs,
  to garnish

VARIATION

Replace the raisins with sultanas.
Add a little grated lemon or
orange rind for added zing.

1 Cut the courgettes into long thin strips. Heat the oil in a large heavy-based frying pan over a medium heat. Add the garlic and fry, stirring constantly, for 2 minutes.

2 Add the courgettes and cook, stirring frequently, or until they just begin to turn brown. Add the vinegar and water. Reduce the heat and simmer for 10 minutes.

3 Meanwhile, drain the anchovies, if canned, or rinse if they are salted. Roughly chop, then use the back of a wooden spoon to mash them to a paste.

4 Stir the anchovies, pine kernels and raisins into the frying pan. Increase the heat and stir until the courgettes are coated in a thin sauce and are tender. Taste and adjust the seasoning, remembering that the anchovies are very salty.

5 Either serve immediately or leave to cool completely, then serve at room temperature. To serve, garnish with fresh parsley sprigs.

NUTRITION	
Calories 90	Sugars 5g
Protein 3g	Fat 4g
Carbohydrate 5g	Saturates 1g

braised fennel

serves four–six

2 lemon slices

3 fennel bulbs

4½ tsp olive oil

3 tbsp butter

4 fresh thyme sprigs or ½ tbsp
   dried thyme

pepper

175 ml/6 fl oz chicken or
   vegetable stock

85 g/3 oz freshly grated
   Parmesan cheese

NUTRITION

Calories 149	Sugars 2g
Protein 6g	Fat 13g
Carbohydrate 2g	Saturates 7g

1 Preheat the oven to 200°C/400°F/
Gas Mark 6. Bring a saucepan of
water to the boil and add the lemon
slices. Slice the fennel lengthways,
then add to the saucepan, return the
water to the boil and simmer for
8 minutes, or until just tender. Drain.

2 Place the oil and butter in a
flameproof casserole over a
medium heat. Swirl the melted mixture
around so the base and sides of the
casserole are well coated.

COOK'S TIP

This is an ideal way to serve
older fennel bulbs, but will not
improve any that have been
stored too long and dried out.

3 Add the fennel slices and stir until
coated. Add the thyme and
season with pepper to taste. Pour in
the stock and sprinkle the Parmesan
cheese over the top.

4 Bake in the preheated oven for
25–30 minutes, or until the
fennel has absorbed the stock and is
tender and the cheese has melted and
become golden brown. Serve
immediately.

steamed lotus rice

serves four

2 lotus leaves

4 Chinese shiitake mushrooms

175 g/6 oz long-grain rice

1 cinnamon stick

6 cardamom pods

4 cloves

1 tsp salt

2 eggs

1 tbsp vegetable oil

2 spring onions, chopped

1 tbsp soy sauce

2 tbsp sherry

1 tsp sugar

1 tsp sesame oil

NUTRITION

Calories 163	Sugars 0.1g
Protein 5g	Fat 6g
Carbohydrate 2.1g	Saturates 1g

1 Unfold the lotus leaves and cut along the fold to divide each leaf in half. Lay on a baking sheet and pour over enough hot water to cover. Leave to soak for 30 minutes, or until softened.

2 Meanwhile, place the mushrooms in a bowl, cover with warm water and leave to soak for 20–25 minutes.

3 Bring a saucepan of water to the boil. Add the rice, cinnamon stick, cardamoms, cloves and salt, return to the boil and cook for 10 minutes – the rice should be partially cooked. Drain thoroughly and remove the cinnamon stick. Place the rice in a bowl.

4 Beat the eggs lightly. Heat the oil in a preheated wok and cook the eggs quickly, stirring until set. Remove and reserve.

5 Drain the mushrooms, squeezing out the excess water. Remove the tough stems and chop the mushrooms. Stir into the rice with the egg, spring onions, soy sauce, sherry, sugar and sesame oil.

6 Drain the lotus leaves and divide the rice into 4 portions. Place a portion in the centre of each leaf and fold up to form a parcel. Place in a steamer, cover and steam over simmering water for 20 minutes. To serve, cut the tops of the lotus leaves open to expose the rice inside.

bamboo with spinach

serves four

3 tbsp peanut oil

225 g/8 oz fresh spinach, chopped

175 g/6 oz canned bamboo shoots,
  drained and rinsed

1 garlic clove, crushed

2 fresh red chillies, sliced

pinch of ground cinnamon

300 ml/10 fl oz vegetable stock

pinch of sugar

pinch of salt

1 tbsp light soy sauce

NUTRITION

Calories 105	Sugars 1g
Protein 3g	Fat 9g
Carbohydrate 3g	Saturates 2g

COOK'S TIP

Fresh bamboo shoots are rarely
available in the West. Canned
bamboo shoots are quite
satisfactory, because they are
used to provide a crunchy
texture, rather than for their
flavour, which is quite bland.

1 Heat the oil in a preheated wok
or large heavy-based frying pan,
swirling the oil around the base of the
wok until it is very hot.

2 Add the spinach and bamboo
shoots to the wok and stir-fry for
1 minute.

3 Add the garlic, chillies and
cinnamon to the wok and stir-fry
for a further 30 seconds.

4 Stir in the stock, sugar, salt and
soy sauce, cover and cook over a
medium heat for 5 minutes, or until the
vegetables are cooked through and the
sauce has reduced. (If there is too
much cooking liquid, blend a little
cornflour with double the quantity of
cold water and stir it into the sauce.)
Transfer the bamboo shoots and
spinach to a serving dish and serve.

easy cauliflower & broccoli

serves four

2 baby cauliflowers

225 g/8 oz broccoli

salt and pepper

SAUCE

8 tbsp olive oil

4 tbsp butter or margarine

2 tsp grated fresh root ginger

juice and rind of 2 lemons

5 tbsp chopped fresh coriander

5 tbsp grated Cheddar cheese

COOK'S TIP

Lime or orange could be used instead of the lemon for a fruity and refreshing sauce.

1 Preheat the grill. Cut the cauliflowers in half and the broccoli into very large florets.

2 Cook the cauliflower and broccoli in a saucepan of boiling salted water for 10 minutes. Drain well, transfer to a shallow ovenproof dish and keep warm until required.

3 To make the sauce, place the oil and butter in a frying pan and heat gently until the butter melts.

NUTRITION	
Calories 433	Sugars 2g
Protein 8g	Fat 44g
Carbohydrate 3g	Saturates 9g

4 Add the ginger, lemon juice, lemon rind and chopped coriander and simmer for 2–3 minutes, stirring occasionally.

5 Season the sauce with salt and pepper to taste, then pour over the vegetables in the dish and sprinkle the cheese on top.

6 Cook under the hot grill for 2–3 minutes, or until the cheese is bubbling and golden brown. Leave to cool for 1–2 minutes, then serve.

mushroom salad

serves four

150 g/5½ oz button mushrooms

4 tbsp virgin olive oil

1 tbsp lemon juice

5 canned anchovy fillets,
    drained and chopped

salt and pepper

1 tbsp fresh marjoram, to garnish

NUTRITION

Calories 121	Sugars 0.1g
Protein 13g	Fat 13g
Carbohydrate 0.1g	Saturates 2g

COOK'S TIP

Do not season the mushroom
salad with salt until the very last
minute because it will cause the
mushrooms to blacken and the
juices to leak. The result will not
be so tasty, because the full
flavours won't be absorbed and
it will also look very unattractive.

1 Gently wipe each mushroom with a damp cloth or damp kitchen paper in order to remove any dirt.

2 Slice the mushrooms thinly, using a sharp knife, and place in a bowl.

3 To make the dressing, whisk the olive oil and lemon juice together in a small bowl.

4 Pour the dressing mixture over the mushrooms. Toss together so that the mushrooms are completely coated with the lemon juice and oil.

5 Stir the chopped anchovy fillets into the mushrooms. Season the mixture with pepper to taste and garnish with the fresh marjoram.

6 Leave the mushroom salad to stand at room temperature for 5 minutes before serving to allow all the flavours to be absorbed.

7 Season the mushroom salad with a little salt (see Cook's Tip), then serve immediately.

mixed leaf salad

serves four

½ head frisée

½ head oak leaf lettuce or
    quattro stagione

few leaves of radicchio

1 head chicory

25 g/1 oz rocket leaves

few fresh basil or flat-leaf
    parsley sprigs

edible flowers, to garnish (optional)

FRENCH DRESSING

1 tbsp white wine vinegar

pinch of sugar

½ tsp Dijon mustard

3 tbsp extra virgin olive oil

salt and pepper

COOK'S TIP

Violets, hardy geraniums, nasturtiums, chive flowers and pot marigolds add vibrant colours and a sweet flavour to this salad. Use it as a centrepiece at a dinner party, or to liven up a simple everyday meal.

1 Tear the frisée, oak leaf lettuce and radicchio into pieces. Place the salad leaves in a large serving bowl or individual bowls, if you prefer.

2 Cut the chicory into diagonal slices and add to the bowl with the rocket leaves and basil.

3 To make the dressing, beat the vinegar, sugar and mustard together in a small bowl until the sugar has dissolved. Gradually beat in the oil until the dressing is creamy and thoroughly mixed. Season to taste with salt and pepper.

4 Pour the dressing over the salad and toss thoroughly. Sprinkle a mixture of edible flowers over the top and serve.

NUTRITION	
Calories 51	Sugars 0.1g
Protein 0.1g	Fat 6g
Carbohydrate 1g	Saturates 0.4g

sesame seed salad

serves four

1 large aubergine

salt and pepper

3 tbsp tahini

juice and rind of 1 lemon

1 garlic clove, crushed

pinch of paprika

1 tbsp chopped fresh coriander

Little Gem lettuce leaves

TO GARNISH

pimiento strips

lemon wedges

toasted sesame seeds

NUTRITION

Calories 89	Sugars 1g
Protein 3g	Fat 8g
Carbohydrate 1g	Saturates 1g

1 Cut the aubergine in half, place in a colander and sprinkle with salt. Leave to stand for 30 minutes to allow the juices to drain. Rinse thoroughly under cold running water and drain well. Pat dry with kitchen paper.

2 Preheat the oven to 230°C/450°F/ Gas Mark 8. Place the aubergine halves, skin-side uppermost, on an oiled baking sheet. Cook in the preheated oven for 10–15 minutes. Leave to cool.

3 When the aubergine is cool enough to handle, cut it into cubes and reserve until required.

4 Mix the tahini, lemon juice, lemon rind, garlic, paprika and chopped coriander together in a medium-sized bowl. Season to taste with salt and pepper and stir in the aubergine cubes.

5 Line a serving dish with lettuce leaves and spoon the aubergine cubes into the centre. Garnish the salad with pimiento slices, lemon wedges and toasted sesame seeds and serve immediately.

cool cucumber salad

serves four

225 g/8 oz cucumber

1 fresh green chilli, finely chopped
(optional)

DRESSING

fresh coriander leaves,
finely chopped

2 tbsp lemon juice

½ tsp salt

1 tsp sugar

TO GARNISH

fresh mint sprigs

red pepper strips

COOK'S TIP

For the best results you can
use a vegetable peeler to thinly
slice the cucumber.

NUTRITION

Calories 11	Sugars 2g
Protein 0.4g	Fat 0g
Carbohydrate 2g	Saturates 0g

1 Slice the cucumber thinly and arrange the slices on a round serving plate.

2 Sprinkle the chopped chilli, if using, over the cucumber.

3 To make the dressing, mix the chopped coriander, lemon juice, salt and sugar together.

4 Place the cucumber in the refrigerator and leave to chill for at least 1 hour, or until required. When ready to serve, transfer the cucumber to a serving dish. Pour the salad dressing over the cucumber just before serving and garnish with fresh mint sprigs and red pepper strips.

italian mozzarella salad

serves six

200 g/7 oz fresh baby spinach

125 g/4½ oz watercress

125 g/4½ oz mozzarella cheese

225 g/8 oz cherry tomatoes

2 tsp balsamic vinegar

4½ tsp extra virgin olive oil

salt and pepper

NUTRITION

Calories 79	Sugars 2g
Protein 4g	Fat 6g
Carbohydrate 2g	Saturates 2g

1 Rinse the spinach and watercress under cold running water and drain thoroughly on kitchen paper. Remove any tough stalks. Place the spinach and watercress leaves in a large serving dish.

2 Cut the mozzarella into small pieces and sprinkle them over the spinach and watercress leaves.

3 Cut the cherry tomatoes in half and sprinkle them over the salad.

4 Sprinkle over the balsamic vinegar and oil and season to taste with salt and pepper. Toss the mixture together to coat the leaves. Serve immediately or leave to chill in the refrigerator until required.

lobster salad

serves two

2 raw lobster tails

radicchio leaves

LEMON-DILL MAYONNAISE

1 large lemon

1 large egg yolk

½ tsp Dijon mustard

150 ml/5 fl oz olive oil

1 tbsp chopped fresh dill

salt and pepper

TO GARNISH

lemon wedges

fresh dill sprigs

NUTRITION

Calories 487	Sugars 2g
Protein 24g	Fat 42g
Carbohydrate 2g	Saturates 6g

1 To make the Lemon-Dill Mayonnaise, finely grate the lemon rind and squeeze the juice. Beat the egg yolk in a small bowl and beat in the mustard and 1 teaspoon of the lemon juice.

2 Using a balloon whisk or electric mixer, beat in the oil, drop by drop, or until a thick mayonnaise forms. Stir in half the lemon rind and 1 tablespoon of the juice.

3 Season with salt and pepper, and add more lemon juice if desired. Stir in the dill and cover with clingfilm. Chill in the refrigerator until required.

4 Bring a large saucepan of lightly salted water to the boil. Add the lobster tails, return to the boil and cook for 6 minutes, or until the flesh is opaque and the shells are red. Drain immediately and leave to cool.

5 Remove the lobster flesh from the shells and cut into bite-sized pieces. Arrange the radicchio leaves on individual serving plates and top with the lobster flesh. Place a spoonful of the Lemon-Dill Mayonnaise on the side. Garnish with lemon wedges and fresh dill sprigs and serve.

smoked trout & apple salad

serves four

2 orange-red dessert apples

2 tbsp French Dressing
(see page 85)

½ bunch watercress

1 smoked trout, about 175 g/6 oz

HORSERADISH DRESSING

125 ml/4 fl oz low-fat natural yogurt

½–1 tsp lemon juice

1 tbsp horseradish sauce

milk (optional)

salt and pepper

TO GARNISH

1 tbsp snipped fresh chives

fresh chive flowers (optional)

NUTRITION

Calories 133	Sugars 11g
Protein 12g	Fat 5g
Carbohydrate 11g	Saturates 1g

1 Leaving the skin on, cut the apples into quarters and remove the cores. Slice the apples into a bowl and toss in the French Dressing to prevent them turning brown.

2 Break the watercress into sprigs and arrange on 4 serving plates.

3 Skin the trout and take out the bones. Carefully remove any fine bones that remain, using your fingers or tweezers. Flake the trout into fairly large pieces and arrange with the apple between the watercress.

4 To make the Horseradish Dressing, whisk all the ingredients together, adding a little milk if too thick, then drizzle over the trout. Sprinkle the snipped chives and flowers, if using, over the trout and serve.

mozzarella & tomato salad

serves four–six

450 g/1 lb cherry tomatoes

4 spring onions

125 ml/4 fl oz extra virgin olive oil

2 tbsp balsamic vinegar

salt and pepper

200 g/7 oz buffalo mozzarella
   (see Cook's Tip), cut into cubes

15 g/½ oz fresh flat-leaf parsley

25 g/1 oz fresh basil leaves

NUTRITION

Calories 295	Sugars 3g
Protein 9g	Fat 27g
Carbohydrate 3g	Saturates 7g

1 Using a sharp knife, cut the tomatoes in half and place them in a large bowl. Trim the spring onions and finely chop both the green and white parts, then add to the bowl.

2 Pour in the oil and vinegar and use your hands to toss together. Season to taste with salt and pepper, add the mozzarella and toss again. Cover with clingfilm and leave to chill in the refrigerator for 4 hours.

3 Remove the salad from the refrigerator 10 minutes before serving. Finely chop the parsley and add to the salad. Tear the basil leaves and sprinkle them over the salad. Toss all the ingredients together again. Adjust the seasoning and serve.

COOK'S TIP

For the best flavour, buy buffalo mozzarella – *mozzarella di bufala* – rather than the factory-made cow's milk version. This salad would also look good made with bocconcini, which are small balls of mozzarella. Find them in Italian delicatessens.

capri salad

serves four

2 beef tomatoes

125 g/4½ oz mozzarella cheese

12 black olives

8 fresh basil leaves

1 tbsp balsamic vinegar

1 tbsp extra virgin olive oil

salt and pepper

fresh basil leaves, to garnish

NUTRITION

Calories 95		Sugars 3g
Protein 3g		Fat 8g
Carbohydrate 3g		Saturates 3g

COOK'S TIP

Beef tomatoes are excellent both cooked and raw because they have a good flavour. When buying tomatoes, always look for ones that are firm to the touch and have a bright red colour.

1 Preheat the grill. Cut the tomatoes into thin slices.

2 Drain the mozzarella, if necessary, and cut into slices.

3 Stone the black olives and slice them into rings.

4 Layer the tomatoes, mozzarella slices, olives and basil leaves in a stack, finishing with a layer of cheese on top.

5 Place each stack under the hot grill for 2–3 minutes, or just long enough to melt the mozzarella.

6 Drizzle over the vinegar and oil and season to taste with a little salt and pepper.

7 Transfer to individual serving plates and garnish with fresh basil leaves. Serve immediately.

grapefruit & cheese salad

serves four

½ cos lettuce

½ oak leaf lettuce

2 pink grapefruit

2 ripe avocados

175 g/6 oz dolcelatte cheese,
   thinly sliced

fresh basil sprigs, to garnish

DRESSING

4 tbsp olive oil

1 tbsp white wine vinegar

salt and pepper

NUTRITION

Calories 390	Sugars 3g
Protein 13g	Fat 36g
Carbohydrate 4g	Saturates 13g

1 Arrange the lettuce leaves on 4 individual serving plates.

2 Remove the peel and pith from the grapefruit with a sharp serrated knife, catching the grapefruit juice in a bowl.

3 Segment the grapefruit by cutting down each side of the membrane. Remove all the membrane. Arrange the segments on the serving plates.

COOK'S TIP

Pink grapefruit segments make a very attractive colour combination with the avocados, but ordinary grapefruit will work just as well. To help avocados to ripen, keep them at room temperature in a brown paper bag.

4 Peel, stone and slice the avocados, dipping them in the grapefruit juice to prevent them turning brown. Arrange the slices on the salad with the dolcelatte cheese.

5 To make the dressing, mix any remaining grapefruit juice, oil and wine vinegar together. Season to taste with salt and pepper and mix thoroughly to combine.

6 Drizzle the dressing over the salads. Garnish with fresh basil sprigs and serve immediately.

Meat & Poultry

Meat and poultry dishes minus our beloved high-carbohydrate components need not be uninspiring or unsatisfying, as these recipes will soon reveal. Here, plain grills and barbecues are transformed by first marinating in spices, herbs and citrus juices, vinegars or wine, which not only boosts the flavour but also tenderizes the flesh. All that is required is a little advance preparation – the cooking takes just a few minutes.

Other recipes make clever use of stuffings and wrappings, for added flavour interest, such as lean pork stuffed with a Parmesan and basil filling, wrapped in Parma ham, and pieces of tender turkey breast stuffed with soft cheese and sage, wrapped in bacon.

Fruit is also put to creative use in this chapter – ham is paired with spiced apple, duck with piquant raspberries and chicken with sweet-scented mango.

beef in barolo

serves four

4 tbsp sunflower oil

1 kg/2 lb 4 oz piece boned rolled rib
of beef, or piece of silverside

2 garlic cloves, crushed

4 shallots, sliced

1 tsp chopped fresh rosemary

1 tsp chopped fresh oregano

2 celery sticks, sliced

1 large carrot, diced

2 whole cloves

1 bottle Barolo wine

freshly grated nutmeg

salt and pepper

cooked vegetables, such as broccoli
and carrots, to serve

NUTRITION

Calories 744	Sugars 1g
Protein 66g	Fat 43g
Carbohydrate 1g	Saturates 16g

1 Heat the oil in a flameproof casserole and brown the meat all over. Remove the meat from the casserole and reserve.

2 Add the garlic, shallots, herbs, celery, carrot and cloves to the casserole and fry for 5 minutes.

3 Replace the meat on top of the vegetables. Pour in the wine, then cover and simmer gently for 2 hours, or until tender. Remove the meat from the casserole, leave to rest before slicing and keep warm.

4 Press the remaining contents of the casserole through a sieve or process in a food processor, adding a little hot beef stock if necessary. Season with nutmeg, salt and pepper.

5 Serve the meat with the sauce and accompanied by cooked vegetables, such as broccoli and carrots.

COOK'S TIP

Barolo is a famous wine from the Piedmont area of Italy. If it is unavailable, choose another full-bodied red wine instead.

beef with wild mushrooms

serves four

4 fillet or sirloin steaks

2 tbsp butter

1–2 garlic cloves, crushed

150 g/5½ oz mixed wild
   mushrooms

2 tbsp chopped fresh parsley

TO SERVE

salad leaves

cherry tomatoes, halved

NUTRITION

Calories 414		Sugars 0g
Protein 49g		Fat 24g
Carbohydrate 1g		Saturates 13g

COOK'S TIP

Wild mushrooms, such as
shiitake, oyster and chanterelle,
are now readily available in
supermarkets. Look for boxes of
mixed wild mushrooms, which
are usually cheaper than buying
the different types individually.

1 Preheat the barbecue. Place the steaks on a chopping board and, using a sharp knife, cut a pocket in the side of each steak.

2 To make the stuffing, heat the butter in a frying pan, add the garlic and cook gently for 1 minute.

3 Add the mushrooms to the frying pan and cook for 4–6 minutes, or until tender. Stir in the parsley.

4 Divide the mushroom mixture into 4 and insert a portion into the pocket of each steak. Seal the pocket closed with a cocktail stick. If preparing ahead, allow the mixture to cool before stuffing the steaks.

5 Barbecue the steaks over hot coals, searing the meat over the hottest part of the barbecue for 2 minutes on each side. Move the steaks to an area with slightly less intense heat (usually the sides) and barbecue for a further 4–10 minutes on each side, depending on how well done you like your steaks.

6 Transfer the steaks to serving plates and remove the cocktail sticks. Serve with salad leaves and cherry tomatoes.

beef, tomato & olive kebabs

makes eight

450 g/1 lb rump or sirloin steak

16 cherry tomatoes

16 large stoned green olives

salt and pepper

BASTE

4 tbsp olive oil

1 tbsp sherry vinegar

1 garlic clove, crushed

FRESH TOMATO RELISH

1 tbsp olive oil

½ red onion, finely chopped

1 garlic clove, chopped

6 plum tomatoes, peeled, deseeded
    and chopped

2 stoned green olives, sliced

1 tbsp chopped fresh parsley

1 tbsp lemon juice

1 Preheat the barbecue. Trim any fat from the beef and cut into 24 pieces.

2 Thread the meat onto 8 presoaked wooden skewers, alternating the pieces with cherry tomatoes and olives.

3 To make the baste, combine the oil, vinegar, garlic, salt and pepper to taste in a bowl.

4 To make the relish, heat the oil in a small saucepan. Add the onion and garlic and fry for 3–4 minutes, or until softened. Add the tomatoes and olives and cook for 2–3 minutes, or until the tomatoes are softened slightly. Stir in the parsley and lemon juice and season to taste. Reserve.

NUTRITION	
Calories 166	Sugars 1g
Protein 12g	Fat 12g
Carbohydrate 1g	Saturates 3g

5 Barbecue the skewers on an oiled rack over hot coals for 5–10 minutes, basting and turning frequently. Serve with the tomato relish.

103

escalopes and italian sausage

serves four

1 tbsp olive oil

6 canned anchovy fillets, drained

1 tbsp capers, drained

1 tbsp chopped fresh
rosemary leaves

finely grated rind and juice of
1 orange

75 g/2¾ oz Italian sausage, diced

3 tomatoes, peeled and chopped

4 turkey or veal escalopes, about
125 g/4½ oz each

salt and pepper

NUTRITION

Calories 233	Sugars 1g
Protein 28g	Fat 13g
Carbohydrate 1g	Saturates 1g

1 Heat the oil in a large frying pan. Add the anchovies, capers, rosemary, orange rind and juice, Italian sausage and tomatoes and cook for 5–6 minutes, stirring occasionally.

2 Meanwhile, place the turkey escalopes between sheets of greaseproof paper. Pound the meat with a meat mallet or the end of a rolling pin to flatten it.

3 Add the meat to the mixture in the frying pan. Season to taste with salt and pepper, cover and cook for 3–5 minutes on each side, slightly longer if the meat is thicker.

4 Transfer to serving plates and serve immediately.

COOK'S TIP

Try using 4 minute-steaks, slightly flattened, instead of the turkey or veal. Cook them for 2–3 minutes on top of the sauce in the frying pan.

meatball brochettes

serves four

25 g/1 oz bulgar wheat
350 g/12 oz lean fresh beef mince
1 onion, finely chopped (optional)
1 tbsp tomato ketchup
1 tbsp brown fruity sauce
1 tbsp chopped fresh parsley
beaten egg, to bind (optional)
8 cherry tomatoes
8 button mushrooms
vegetable oil, for basting
assorted cooked vegetables,
    to serve

NUTRITION

Calories 120	Sugars 2g
Protein 17g	Fat 5g
Carbohydrate 2g	Saturates 2g

1 Preheat the barbecue. Place the bulgar wheat in a heatproof bowl and cover with boiling water. Leave to soak for 20 minutes, or until softened. Drain well and leave to cool.

2 Place the soaked wheat, beef, onion, if using, ketchup, brown fruity sauce and chopped parsley together in a large bowl and mix until all the ingredients are well combined. Add a little beaten egg if necessary to bind the mixture together.

3 Using your hands, shape the meat mixture into 18 even-sized balls. Leave to chill in the refrigerator for 30 minutes.

4 Thread the meatballs onto 8 pre-soaked wooden skewers, alternating them with the cherry tomatoes and button mushrooms.

5 Brush the brochettes with a little oil and cook over hot coals, turning occasionally and brushing with a little more oil if the meat begins to dry out, for 10 minutes, or until cooked through.

6 Transfer to warmed serving plates and serve with vegetables.

minced lamb with peas

serves four

6 tbsp sunflower oil

1 onion, sliced

2 fresh red chillies, chopped

1 bunch fresh coriander, chopped

2 tomatoes, chopped

1 tsp salt

1 tsp finely chopped fresh
   root ginger

1 garlic clove, crushed

1 tsp chilli powder

450 g/1 lb fresh lean lamb mince

100 g/3½ oz peas

2 fresh green chillies, to garnish

COOK'S TIP

The flavour of garlic varies
in strength depending on how
it is prepared. For instance,
a whole garlic clove added
to a dish will give it the
flavour but not the pungency
of garlic; a halved clove will
add a little 'bite'; a finely
chopped garlic clove will
release most of its flavour,
and a crushed clove will
release all of the flavour.

1 Heat the oil in a medium-sized saucepan. Add the onion slices and fry until golden brown, stirring.

2 Add the red chillies, half of the chopped coriander and the tomatoes to the saucepan and reduce the heat to a simmer.

3 Add the salt, ginger, garlic and chilli powder to the mixture in the saucepan and stir well.

4 Add the lamb mince to the saucepan and stir-fry the mixture for 7–10 minutes.

5 Add the peas to the mixture in the saucepan and cook for a further 3–4 minutes, stirring occasionally.

6 Transfer to serving plates and garnish with green chillies and the remaining coriander.

NUTRITION

Calories 357	Sugars 3g
Protein 25g	Fat 26g
Carbohydrate 6g	Saturates 6g

107

moroccan lamb kebabs

serves four

450 g/1 lb lean lamb

1 lemon

1 red onion

4 small courgettes

couscous, to serve (see Cook's Tip)

MARINADE

grated rind and juice of 1 lemon

2 tbsp olive oil

1 garlic clove, crushed

1 fresh red chilli, sliced (optional)

1 tsp ground cinnamon

1 tsp ground ginger

½ tsp ground cumin

½ tsp ground coriander

COOK'S TIP

Serve these kebabs with couscous. Allowing 55 g/2 oz couscous per person, soak the couscous in cold water for 20 minutes, or until softened. Drain and steam for 10 minutes, or until piping hot.

1 Cut the lamb into even, bite-sized chunks, and place in a large non-metallic dish.

2 To make the marinade, mix the lemon rind and juice, oil, garlic, chilli, if using, ground cinnamon, ginger, cumin and coriander together.

3 Pour the marinade over the lamb and toss to coat. Cover and leave to marinate in the refrigerator for at least 2 hours, or preferably overnight.

4 Preheat the barbecue. Cut the lemon into 8 pieces. Cut the onion into wedges, then separate each wedge into 2 pieces.

5 Using a canelle knife or potato peeler, cut thin strips of peel from the courgettes, then cut the courgettes into even-sized chunks.

NUTRITION

Calories 348	Sugars 2g
Protein 30g	Fat 24g
Carbohydrate 2g	Saturates 10g

6 Remove the meat from the marinade, reserving the liquid for basting. Thread the meat onto metal skewers, alternating with the onion, lemon and courgette.

7 Cook over hot coals for 8–10 minutes, turning and basting with the marinade. Serve on a bed of couscous (see Cook's Tip).

lamb with bay & lemon

serves four

4 lamb chops

1 tbsp sunflower oil

15 g/½ oz butter

150 ml/5 fl oz white wine

150 ml/5 fl oz lamb or
   vegetable stock

2 bay leaves

pared rind of 1 lemon

salt and pepper

NUTRITION

Calories 268	Sugars 0.2g
Protein 24g	Fat 16g
Carbohydrate 0.2g	Saturates 7g

COOK'S TIP

Your local butcher will offer you good advice on how to prepare the lamb noisettes, if you are wary of preparing them yourself.

1 Using a sharp knife, carefully remove the bone from each lamb chop, keeping the meat intact. Alternatively, ask the butcher to prepare the lamb noisettes for you.

2 Shape the meat into rounds and secure with a length of string.

3 Heat the oil and butter together in a large frying pan until the mixture begins to froth.

4 Add the lamb noisettes to the frying pan and cook for 2–3 minutes on each side, or until browned all over.

5 Remove the frying pan from the heat, remove the meat, drain off all of the excess fat and discard. Place the noisettes back in the frying pan.

6 Return the frying pan to the heat. Add the wine, stock, bay leaves and lemon rind and cook for 20–25 minutes, or until the lamb is tender. Season the lamb and sauce to taste with a little salt and pepper.

7 Transfer to serving plates. Remove the string from each noisette and serve with the sauce.

red wine lamb skewers

serves four

450 g/1 lb lean lamb

12 pearl onions or shallots

12 button mushrooms

MARINADE

150 ml/5 fl oz red wine

4 tbsp olive oil

2 tbsp brandy (optional)

1 onion, sliced

1 bay leaf

fresh thyme sprig

2 fresh parsley sprigs

TO SERVE

salad leaves

cherry tomatoes

1 Carefully trim away any excess fat from the lamb. Cut the lamb into large pieces.

2 To make the marinade, mix the wine, oil, brandy, if using, onion, bay leaf, thyme and parsley sprigs together in a non-metallic dish.

NUTRITION

Calories 353	Sugars 5g
Protein 24g	Fat 21g
Carbohydrate 7g	Saturates 6g

3 Add the meat and toss to coat. Cover and leave to marinate in the refrigerator for at least 2 hours, or preferably overnight.

4 Preheat the barbecue. Bring a saucepan of water to a rolling boil, drop in the unpeeled pearl onions and blanch them for 3 minutes. Drain and refresh under cold water, and then drain again. Trim the onions and remove their skins.

5 Remove the meat from the marinade, reserving the liquid for basting. Thread the meat onto metal skewers, alternating with the pearl onions and mushrooms.

6 Cook the kebabs over hot coals for 8–10 minutes, turning and basting the meat and vegetables with the reserved marinade a few times.

7 Transfer the kebabs to warmed serving plates and serve with salad leaves and cherry tomatoes.

lamb cutlets with rosemary

serves four

8 lamb cutlets

5 tbsp olive oil

2 tbsp lemon juice

1 garlic clove, crushed

½ tsp lemon pepper

salt

8 fresh rosemary sprigs

SALAD

4 tomatoes, sliced

4 spring onions, diagonally sliced

DRESSING

2 tbsp olive oil

1 tbsp lemon juice

1 garlic clove, chopped

¼ tsp finely chopped fresh rosemary

NUTRITION

Calories 560	Sugars 1g
Protein 48g	Fat 40g
Carbohydrate 1g	Saturates 13g

1 Preheat the barbecue. Trim the lamb by cutting away the flesh to expose the tips of the bones.

2 Place the oil, lemon juice, garlic, lemon, pepper and salt in a shallow non-metallic dish and whisk with a fork to combine.

3 Lay the rosemary sprigs in the dish and place the lamb on top. Cover and leave to marinate for at least 1 hour, turning the lamb cutlets once.

4 Remove the chops from the marinade and wrap foil around the exposed bones to stop them from burning.

5 Place the rosemary sprigs on the rack and place the lamb on top. Barbecue over hot coals for 10–15 minutes, turning once.

6 Meanwhile, make the salad and dressing. Arrange the tomatoes on a serving dish and sprinkle the spring onions on top. Place all the ingredients for the dressing in a screw-top jar, shake well and pour over the salad. Serve with the barbecued lamb cutlets.

lamb with olives

serves four

1.25 kg/2 lb 12 oz boned leg
of lamb

6 tbsp olive oil

2 garlic cloves, crushed

1 onion, sliced

1 small fresh red chilli, deseeded
and finely chopped

175 ml/6 fl oz dry white wine

175 g/6 oz stoned black olives

salt

1 fresh flat-leaf parsley sprig,
to garnish

NUTRITION

Calories 577	Sugars 1g
Protein 62g	Fat 33g
Carbohydrate 1g	Saturates 10g

1 Preheat the oven to 180°C/350°F/Gas Mark 4. Cut the lamb into 2.5-cm/1-inch cubes with a sharp knife.

2 Heat the oil in a frying pan over a medium heat. Add the garlic, onion and chilli and fry for 5 minutes.

3 Add the meat and wine and cook for a further 5 minutes.

4 Stir in the olives, then transfer the mixture to a casserole dish. Cook in the preheated oven for 1 hour 20 minutes, or until the meat is tender. Season with salt to taste. Transfer to a serving plate, garnish with a parsley sprig and serve.

lamb & anchovies with thyme

serves four

1 tbsp sunflower oil

15 g/½ oz butter

600 g/1 lb 5 oz lamb (shoulder or
　leg), cut into 2.5-cm/
　1-inch chunks

4 garlic cloves, peeled

3 fresh thyme sprigs, stalks removed

6 canned anchovy fillets

150 ml/5 fl oz red wine

150 ml/5 fl oz lamb or
　vegetable stock

1 tsp sugar

50 g/1¾ oz black olives, stoned
　and halved

2 tbsp chopped fresh parsley,
　to garnish

NUTRITION

Calories 577	Sugars 1g
Protein 62g	Fat 33g
Carbohydrate 1g	Saturates 10g

COOK'S TIP

This dish is excellent served
with Chargrilled Vegetables
(see page 189).

1 Heat the oil and butter in a large frying pan. Add the lamb and cook for 4–5 minutes, stirring, or until the meat is browned all over.

2 Using a pestle and mortar, grind the garlic, thyme and anchovies together to make a smooth paste.

3 Add the wine and stock to the frying pan. Stir in the garlic and anchovy paste together with the sugar.

4 Bring the mixture to the boil, reduce the heat, cover and leave to simmer for 30–40 minutes, or until the lamb is tender. For the last 10 minutes of the cooking time, remove the lid in order to allow the sauce to reduce slightly.

5 Stir the olives into the sauce and mix to combine.

6 Transfer the lamb and its sauce to a serving bowl and garnish with chopped fresh parsley. Serve.

pork stir-fry with vegetables

serves four

2 tbsp vegetable oil

2 garlic cloves, crushed

1-cm/½-inch piece fresh root ginger,
   cut into slivers

350 g/12 oz lean pork fillet,
   thinly sliced

1 carrot, cut into thin strips

1 red pepper, deseeded and diced

1 fennel bulb, sliced

25 g/1 oz water chestnuts, halved

85 g/3 oz beansprouts

2 tbsp rice wine

300 m/ 10 fl oz pork or
   chicken stock

pinch of dark brown sugar

1 tsp cornflour

2 tsp water

1 Heat the oil in a preheated wok. Add the garlic, ginger and pork. Stir-fry for 1–2 minutes, or until the meat is sealed.

2 Add the carrot, pepper, fennel and water chestnuts and stir-fry for 2–3 minutes.

NUTRITION

Calories 216	Sugars 3g
Protein 19g	Fat 12g
Carbohydrate 5g	Saturates 3g

3 Add the beansprouts and stir-fry for 1 minute. Remove the pork and vegetables and keep warm.

4 Add the rice wine, stock and sugar to the wok. Blend the cornflour to a smooth paste with the water and stir it into the sauce. Bring to the boil, stirring constantly, or until thickened and clear.

5 Return the meat and vegetables to the wok and cook for 1–2 minutes, or until heated through and coated with the sauce. Serve immediately.

VARIATION
Use dry sherry instead of the rice wine if you have difficulty obtaining it.

baked ham with sauce

serves four–six

2–3 kg/4 lb 8 oz–6 lb 8 oz lean
 gammon

2 bay leaves

1–2 onions, quartered

2 carrots, thickly sliced

6 cloves

GLAZE

1 tbsp redcurrant jelly

1 tbsp wholegrain mustard

CUMBERLAND SAUCE

1 orange

3 tbsp redcurrant jelly

2 tbsp lemon or lime juice

2 tbsp orange juice

2–4 tbsp port

1 tbsp wholegrain mustard

TO GARNISH

salad leaves

orange slices

NUTRITION

Calories 414	Sugars 4g
Protein 70g	Fat 13g
Carbohydrate 4g	Saturates 5g

1 Place the meat in a large saucepan. Add the bay leaves, onions, carrots and cloves and cover with cold water. Bring to the boil over a low heat, cover and simmer for half the cooking time. To calculate the cooking time, allow 30 minutes per 500 g/1 lb 2 oz plus 30 minutes.

2 Preheat the oven to 180°C/ 350°F/Gas Mark 4. Drain the meat and remove the skin. Place the meat in a roasting tin and score the fat. To make the glaze, combine the ingredients and spread over the fat. Cook in the oven for the remainder of the cooking time. Baste at least once.

3 To make the sauce, pare the rind from half the orange and cut into strips. Cook in boiling water for 3 minutes. Drain.

4 Place all the remaining sauce ingredients in a small saucepan and heat gently, stirring occasionally, or until the redcurrant jelly dissolves. Add the orange rind strips and simmer gently for a further 3–4 minutes.

5 Slice the gammon and place on a warmed serving platter. Garnish with salad leaves and orange slices and serve with the Cumberland Sauce.

griddled pork with orange sauce

serves four

4 tbsp freshly squeezed orange juice

4 tbsp red wine vinegar

2 garlic cloves, finely chopped

pepper

4 pork steaks, trimmed of all
    visible fat

olive oil, for brushing

GREMOLATA

3 tbsp finely chopped fresh parsley

grated rind of 1 lime

grated rind of ½ lemon

1 garlic clove, very finely chopped

NUTRITION	
Calories 204	Sugars 1g
Protein 26g	Fat 10g
Carbohydrate 2g	Saturates 3g

1 Mix the orange juice, vinegar and garlic together in a shallow, non-metallic dish and season to taste with pepper. Add the pork, turning to coat. Cover and leave in the refrigerator to marinate for up to 3 hours.

2 Meanwhile, mix all the Gremolata ingredients together in a small mixing bowl, cover with clingfilm and leave to chill in the refrigerator until required.

3 Heat a non-stick griddle pan and brush lightly with olive oil. Remove the pork from the marinade, reserving the marinade, add to the pan and cook over a medium–high heat for 5 minutes on each side, or until the juices run clear when the meat is pierced with a skewer.

4 Meanwhile, pour the marinade into a small saucepan and simmer over a medium heat for 5 minutes, or until slightly thickened. Transfer the pork to a serving dish, pour the orange sauce over it and sprinkle with the Gremolata. Serve immediately.

VARIATION

This dish would work equally well with chicken breast portions. Remove the skin from the cooked chicken before serving.

stuffed pork with parma ham

serves four

500 g/1 lb 2 oz piece of lean pork
    fillet, trimmed of excess fat
salt and pepper
small bunch of fresh basil leaves,
    plus extra to garnish
2 tbsp freshly grated Parmesan
    cheese
2 tbsp sun-dried tomato paste
6 thin slices Parma ham
1 tbsp olive oil
radicchio, to serve
OLIVE PASTE
125 g/4 oz stoned black olives
2 garlic cloves, peeled
4 tbsp olive oil

COOK'S TIP

Choose a good lean piece of pork
fillet for the best results.

NUTRITION

Calories 427	Sugars 0g
Protein 31g	Fat 34g
Carbohydrate 0.2g	Saturates 7g

1 Preheat the oven to 190°C/
375°F/Gas Mark 5. Slice the
pork lengthways down the middle,
taking care not to cut all the
way through.

2 Open out the pork and season the
inside with salt and pepper. Lay
the basil leaves down the centre. Mix
the cheese and sun-dried tomato paste
and spread over the basil.

3 Press the pork back together.
Wrap the ham around the pork,
overlapping, to cover. Place on a rack
in a roasting tin, seam-side down, and
brush with oil. Bake in the preheated
oven for 30–40 minutes, depending
on thickness, or until cooked through.
Leave to stand for 10 minutes.

4 To make the Olive Paste, place
all the ingredients in a food
processor or blender and process until
smooth. Alternatively, for a coarser
paste, finely chop the olives and garlic
and mix with the oil.

5 Drain the cooked pork and slice.
Serve with the Olive Paste and
radicchio, garnished with a sprig of
fresh basil.

pork & sage kebabs

serves twelve

450 g/1 lb fresh pork mince

2 tbsp fresh breadcrumbs

1 small onion, very finely chopped

1 tbsp chopped fresh sage

2 tbsp apple sauce

¼ tsp ground nutmeg

salt and pepper

BASTE

3 tbsp olive oil

1 tbsp lemon juice

TO SERVE

mixed salad leaves

6 tbsp thick natural yogurt

NUTRITION

Calories 96	Sugars 0g
Protein 8g	Fat 7g
Carbohydrate 2g	Saturates 2g

1 Place the mince in a large bowl. Add the breadcrumbs, onion, sage, apple sauce, and nutmeg, season to taste and mix until well combined.

2 Using your hands, shape the mixture into balls, about the size of large marbles, and leave to chill in the refrigerator for at least 30 minutes.

3 Preheat the barbecue. Soak 12 small wooden skewers in cold water for 30 minutes. Thread the meatballs onto the skewers.

4 To make the baste, mix the oil and lemon juice in a small bowl, whisking with a fork until blended.

5 Barbecue the kebabs over hot coals for 8–10 minutes, turning and basting until the meat is cooked through.

6 Spoon some of the yogurt over the salad leaves. Serve immediately with the kebabs.

carnitas

serves four–six

1 kg/2 lb 4 oz pork, such as
  lean belly
1 onion, chopped
1 garlic bulb, cut in half
½ tsp ground cumin
2 meat stock cubes
2 bay leaves
salt and pepper
fresh chilli strips, to garnish
salsa of your choice,
  to serve

NUTRITION

Calories 236	Sugars 1g
Protein 36g	Fat 9g
Carbohydrate 3g	Saturates 3g

1 Place the pork in a heavy-based frying pan with the onion, garlic, cumin, stock cubes and bay leaves. Add just enough water to cover. Bring to the boil, then reduce the heat to very low. Skim off the foam and scum that forms on the surface of the liquid.

2 Simmer very gently for 2 hours, or until the meat is cooked through and tender. Remove the frying pan from the heat and leave the meat to cool in the cooking liquid.

3 Remove the meat from the frying pan with a slotted spoon. Cut off any rind (roast separately to make crackling). Cut the meat into bite-sized pieces and season to taste with salt and pepper. Reserve 300 ml/10 fl oz of the cooking liquid.

4 Brown the meat in a heavy-based frying pan for 15 minutes to cook out the fat. Add the reserved cooking liquid and reduce. Cover and cook the meat for a further 15 minutes, turning the meat occasionally.

5 Transfer the meat to a serving dish and garnish with chilli strips. Serve with salsa.

pork with mooli

serves four

4 tbsp vegetable oil

450 g/1 lb pork fillet

1 aubergine

225 g/8 oz mooli

2 garlic cloves, crushed

3 tbsp light soy sauce

2 tbsp sweet chilli sauce

cooked rice or noodles, to serve

NUTRITION

Calories 280	Sugars 1g
Protein 25g	Fat 19g
Carbohydrate 2g	Saturates 4g

COOK'S TIP

Mooli are long white vegetables common in Chinese cooking. Usually grated, they have a milder flavour than red radish. They are generally available in most large supermarkets.

1 Heat 2 tablespoons of the oil in a preheated wok or large heavy-based frying pan.

2 Using a sharp knife, thinly slice the pork into even-sized pieces.

3 Add the slices of pork to the wok and stir-fry for 5 minutes.

4 Using a sharp knife, trim and dice the aubergine. Peel and thinly slice the mooli.

5 Add the remaining vegetable oil to the wok.

6 Add the diced aubergine to the wok together with the garlic and stir-fry for 5 minutes.

7 Add the mooli to the wok and stir-fry for 2 minutes.

8 Stir the soy sauce and sweet chilli sauce into the mixture in the wok and cook until heated through.

9 Transfer the pork to serving bowls and serve immediately.

ham steaks with apple rings

serves four

4 ham steaks, about 175 g/
   6 oz each

1–2 tsp wholegrain mustard

1 tbsp honey

2 tbsp lemon juice

1 tbsp sunflower oil

APPLE RINGS

2 green dessert apples

2 tsp demerara sugar

¼ tsp ground nutmeg

¼ tsp ground cinnamon

¼ tsp ground mixed spice

1–2 tbsp melted butter

NUTRITION	
Calories 358	Sugars 13g
Protein 31g	Fat 21g
Carbohydrate 13g	Saturates 8g

1 Preheat the barbecue. Using a pair of scissors, make a few cuts around the edges of the ham steaks to prevent them curling up as they cook. Spread a little wholegrain mustard over the steaks.

2 Mix the honey, lemon juice and oil together in a bowl.

3 To prepare the Apple Rings, core the apples and cut them into thick slices. Mix the sugar with the spices and press the apple slices in the mixture until well coated on both sides.

4 Cook the ham steaks over hot coals for 3–4 minutes on each side, basting frequently with the honey and lemon mixture.

COOK'S TIP

Ham can be a little salty. If you have time, soak the steaks in cold water for 30–60 minutes before cooking – this process will remove the excess salt.

5 Meanwhile, brush the apple slices with melted butter and cook them over the hot coals, alongside the ham steaks, for 3–4 minutes, turning once, and brushing with melted butter as they cook.

6 Serve the ham steaks with the cooked apple slices.

thai stir-fried chicken

serves four

3 tbsp sesame oil

350 g/12 oz skinless, boneless
   chicken breast, thinly sliced

salt and pepper

8 shallots, sliced

2 garlic cloves, finely chopped

2 tsp grated fresh root ginger

1 fresh green chilli, deseeded and
   finely chopped

1 red pepper, deseeded and
   thinly sliced

1 green pepper, deseeded and
   thinly sliced

3 courgettes, thinly sliced

2 tbsp ground almonds

1 tsp ground cinnamon

1 tbsp oyster sauce

20 g/¾ oz creamed coconut, grated

1 Heat the oil in a preheated wok
   or heavy-based frying pan. Add
the chicken, season to taste with salt
and pepper and stir-fry over a medium
heat for 4 minutes.

2 Add the shallots, garlic, ginger
   and green chilli and stir-fry for a
further 2 minutes.

NUTRITION

Calories 184	Sugars 6g
Protein 24g	Fat 5g
Carbohydrate 8g	Saturates 2g

3 Add the red and green peppers
   and courgettes and stir-fry for
1 minute.

4 Stir in the almonds, cinnamon,
   oyster sauce and creamed
coconut and season to taste with salt
and pepper. Stir-fry for 1 minute to
heat through, then serve immediately.

COOK'S TIP

Creamed coconut is sold in
supermarkets and Thai shops.
It is a useful storecupboard
standby because it adds
richness and depth of flavour.

sweet mango chicken

serves four

1 tbsp sunflower oil

6 skinless, boneless chicken thighs

1 ripe mango

2 garlic cloves, crushed

225 g/8 oz leeks, shredded

100 g/3½ oz beansprouts

150 ml/5 fl oz mango juice

1 tbsp white wine vinegar

2 tbsp clear honey

2 tbsp tomato ketchup

1 tsp cornflour

NUTRITION

Calories 244	Sugars 18g
Protein 27g	Fat 7g
Carbohydrate 2.1g	Saturates 2g

COOK'S TIP

Mango juice is available in jars from most supermarkets and is quite thick and sweet. If it is unavailable, purée and sieve a ripe mango and add a little water to make up the required quantity.

1 Heat the oil in a preheated wok or large frying pan.

2 Cut the chicken into bite-sized cubes, add to the wok and stir-fry over a high heat for 10 minutes, tossing frequently, or until the chicken is cooked through and golden in colour.

3 Peel and slice the mango and add to the wok with the garlic, leeks and beansprouts. Stir-fry for a further 2–3 minutes, or until softened.

4 Mix the mango juice, vinegar, honey, ketchup and cornflour together. Pour into the wok and stir-fry for a further 2 minutes, or until the juices begin to thicken.

5 Transfer to a warmed serving plate and serve immediately.

karahi chicken

serves four

2 tbsp ghee

3 garlic cloves, crushed

1 onion, finely chopped

2 tbsp garam masala

1 tsp coriander seeds, ground

½ tsp dried mint

1 bay leaf

750 g/1 lb 10 oz lean boneless
    chicken, diced

200 ml/7 fl oz chicken stock

1 tbsp chopped fresh coriander

salt

mixed salad, to serve

NUTRITION

Calories 270		Sugars 1g	
Protein 41g		Fat 11g	
Carbohydrate 1g		Saturates 2g	

1 Heat the ghee in a preheated karahi, wok or large heavy-based frying pan. Add the garlic and onion and stir-fry for 4 minutes, or until the onion is golden.

2 Stir in the garam masala, ground coriander, mint and bay leaf.

3 Add the diced chicken and cook over a high heat, stirring occasionally, for 5 minutes. Add the stock, reduce the heat and simmer for 10 minutes, or until the sauce has thickened and the chicken is thoroughly cooked and tender.

4 Stir in the chopped coriander and season with salt to taste, mix well and serve immediately with mixed salad.

COOK'S TIP

It is important always to heat
a karahi or wok before you
add the oil to help maintain
the high temperature.

minty lime chicken

serves six

3 tbsp finely chopped fresh mint

4 tbsp clear honey

4 tbsp lime juice

12 boneless chicken thighs

SAUCE

150 g/5½ oz natural thick yogurt

1 tbsp finely chopped fresh mint

2 tsp finely grated lime rind

mixed salad, to serve

COOK'S TIP

Mint can be grown very
easily in a garden or window
box. It is a useful herb for
marinades and salad dressings.
Other useful herbs to grow
are parsley and basil.

1 Mix the mint, honey and lime
juice together in a bowl.

2 Use cocktail sticks to keep the
chicken thighs in neat shapes and
place in a large non-metallic bowl. Add
the marinade to the chicken and turn
to coat evenly.

VARIATION

Use this marinade for chicken
kebabs, alternating the chicken
with lime and red onion wedges.

3 Cover and leave to marinate in
the refrigerator for at least
30 minutes, or preferably overnight.
Preheat the barbecue or grill to
medium. Cook the chicken over the hot
coals or under the hot grill, turning
frequently and basting with the
marinade, or until the chicken is tender
and the juices run clear when a skewer
is inserted into the thickest part of
the meat.

4 Meanwhile, mix the sauce
ingredients together. Remove the
cocktail sticks from the chicken and
serve immediately with the sauce and
a mixed salad.

NUTRITION

Calories 170	Sugars 12g
Protein 23g	Fat 3g
Carbohydrate 12g	Saturates 1g

chicken & ginger stir-fry

serves four

3 tbsp sunflower oil

700 g/1 lb 9 oz lean skinless, boneless chicken breasts, cut into 5-cm/2-inch strips

3 garlic cloves, crushed

4-cm/1½-inch piece fresh root ginger, cut into strips

1 tsp pomegranate seeds, crushed

½ tsp ground turmeric

1 tsp garam masala

2 fresh green chillies, sliced

½ tsp salt

4 tbsp lemon juice

grated rind of 1 lemon

6 tbsp chopped fresh coriander

125 ml/4 fl oz chicken stock

naan bread, to serve

COOK'S TIP

Stir-frying is perfect for low-fat diets as only a little oil is needed. Cooking the food over a high temperature ensures that food is sealed and cooked quickly to hold in the flavour.

1 Heat the oil in a preheated wok or large frying pan. Add the chicken and stir-fry until golden brown all over. Remove from the wok and reserve.

2 Add the garlic, ginger and pomegranate seeds to the wok and fry in the oil for 1 minute, taking care not to let the garlic burn.

3 Stir in the turmeric, garam masala and chillies, and fry for 30 seconds.

4 Return the chicken to the wok and add the salt, lemon juice, lemon rind, coriander and stock. Stir the chicken well to make sure it is coated in the sauce.

5 Bring the mixture to the boil, then reduce the heat and simmer for 10–15 minutes, or until the chicken is cooked. Serve.

NUTRITION	
Calories 291	Sugars 0g
Protein 41g	Fat 14g
Carbohydrate 0g	Saturates 3g

chicken in banana leaves

serves four–six

1 garlic clove, chopped

1 tsp finely chopped fresh
   root ginger

¼ tsp pepper

2 fresh coriander sprigs

1 tbsp Thai fish sauce

1 tbsp whisky

3 skinless, boneless chicken breasts

2–3 banana leaves, cut into 7.5-cm/
   3-inch squares

sunflower oil, for shallow-frying

chilli dipping sauce, to serve

NUTRITION

Calories 185	Sugars 0g
Protein 18g	Fat 12g
Carbohydrate 0.5g	Saturates 1g

1 Place the garlic, ginger, pepper, coriander, fish sauce and whisky in a mortar and, using a pestle, grind to a smooth paste.

2 Cut the chicken into 2.5-cm/ 1-inch chunks and toss in the paste to coat. Cover and leave to marinate in the refrigerator for 1 hour.

3 Place a piece of chicken on a square of banana leaf and wrap it up like a parcel to enclose the chicken completely. Secure with wooden cocktail sticks or tie with string.

4 Heat a 3-mm/⅛-inch depth of oil in a large heavy-based frying pan until hot.

5 Shallow-fry the parcels for 8–10 minutes, turning them over occasionally. Unwrap the parcels and discard the banana leaves. Serve with a chilli dipping sauce.

COOK'S TIP

To make a sweet chilli dipping sauce to serve with the chicken pieces, mix together equal amounts of chilli sauce and tomato ketchup, then stir in a dash of rice wine to taste.

green salsa chicken breasts

serves four

4 skinless chicken breast fillets

salt and pepper

plain flour, for dusting

2–3 tbsp butter or a mixture of
butter and vegetable oil

450 g/1 lb mild green salsa or
puréed tomatillos

225 ml/8 fl oz chicken stock

1–2 garlic cloves, finely chopped

3–5 tbsp chopped fresh coriander

½ fresh green chilli, deseeded
and chopped

½ tsp ground cumin

TO SERVE

225 ml/8 fl oz soured cream

several cos lettuce leaves, shredded

3–5 spring onions, thinly sliced

roughly chopped fresh coriander

1 Sprinkle the chicken with salt and
pepper, then dredge in flour.
Shake off the excess.

2 Melt the butter or heat the butter
and oil mixture in a large heavy-
based frying pan. Add the chicken and
cook over a medium–high heat,
turning once, or until the fillets are
golden all over, but not quite cooked
through – they will continue to cook
slightly in the sauce. Remove from the
frying pan and reserve.

NUTRITION

Calories 349	Sugars 7g
Protein 34g	Fat 20g
Carbohydrate 10g	Saturates 12g

3 Place the salsa, stock, garlic,
coriander, chilli and cumin in a
saucepan and bring to the boil. Reduce
the heat to a low simmer. Add the
chicken breasts to the sauce, spooning
the sauce over the chicken. Continue to
cook until the chicken is cooked
through and tender.

4 Remove the chicken from the
saucepan and season to taste
with salt and pepper. Serve
immediately with the soured cream,
shredded lettuce, sliced spring onions
and chopped fresh coriander.

chicken with balsamic vinegar

serves four

4 boneless chicken thighs

2 garlic cloves, crushed

200 ml/7 fl oz red wine

3 tbsp white wine vinegar

salt and pepper

1 tbsp sunflower oil

15 g/½ oz butter

4 shallots

3 tbsp balsamic vinegar

4 sprigs fresh thyme

NUTRITION

Calories 148	Sugars 0.2g
Protein 11g	Fat 8g
Carbohydrate 0.2g	Saturates 3g

1 Using a sharp knife, make a few slashes in the skin of the chicken. Brush the chicken with the crushed garlic and place in a non-metallic dish.

2 Pour the wine and vinegar over the chicken and season to taste with salt and pepper. Cover with clingfilm and leave to marinate in the refrigerator overnight.

COOK'S TIP

To make the chicken pieces look a little neater, use wooden skewers to hold them together or secure them with a length of string.

3 Remove the chicken pieces with a slotted spoon, draining well, and reserve the marinade.

4 Heat the oil and butter in a frying pan. Add the shallots and cook, stirring, for 2–3 minutes, or until they begin to soften.

5 Add the chicken pieces to the frying pan and cook for 3–4 minutes, turning, or until browned all over. Reduce the heat and add half of the reserved marinade. Cover and cook for 15–20 minutes, adding more marinade when necessary.

6 Once the chicken is tender, add the vinegar and thyme and cook for a further 4 minutes.

7 Transfer the chicken and marinade to serving plates and serve.

chicken in spicy yogurt

serves four

3 dried red chillies

2 tbsp coriander seeds

2 tsp ground turmeric

2 tsp garam masala

4 garlic cloves, crushed

½ onion, chopped

2.5-cm/1-inch piece fresh root
    ginger, grated

2 tbsp lime juice

1 tsp salt

125 ml/4 fl oz low-fat natural yogurt

1 tbsp sunflower oil

2 kg/4 lb 8 oz skinless chicken,
    cut into 6 pieces, or
    6 chicken portions

fresh mint sprigs, to garnish

TO SERVE

chopped tomatoes

diced cucumber

sliced red onion

raita

NUTRITION

Calories 74	Sugars 2g
Protein 9g	Fat 4g
Carbohydrate 2g	Saturates 1g

1 Grind the chillies, coriander seeds, turmeric, garam masala, garlic, onion, ginger, lime juice and salt together in a pestle and mortar.

2 Gently heat a frying pan and add the spice mixture. Stir until fragrant, about 2 minutes, and turn into a shallow non-metallic dish.

3 Add the yogurt and oil to the spice paste and mix well.

4 Make 3 slashes in the flesh of each piece of chicken. Add the chicken to the yogurt and spice mixture and coat the pieces in the marinade. Cover and chill for at least 4 hours. Remove the dish from the refrigerator and leave covered at room temperature for 30 minutes before cooking.

5 Preheat the barbecue. Wrap the chicken pieces in foil, sealing well so the juices cannot escape.

6 Cook the chicken over a very hot barbecue for 15 minutes, turning once. Remove the foil and cook for a further 5 minutes.

7 Garnish the chicken with mint sprigs and serve with tomatoes, cucumber, onion and raita.

jerk chicken

serves four

4 lean chicken portions

1 bunch spring onions

1–2 fresh Scotch Bonnet
chillies, deseeded

1 garlic clove

5-cm/2-inch piece fresh root ginger,
roughly chopped

½ tsp dried thyme

½ tsp paprika

¼ tsp ground allspice

pinch of ground cinnamon

pinch of ground cloves

4 tbsp white wine vinegar

3 tbsp light soy sauce

pepper

1 Place the chicken portions in a shallow non-metallic dish.

2 Place the spring onions, chillies, garlic, ginger, thyme, paprika, allspice, cinnamon, cloves, vinegar, soy sauce and pepper to taste in a food processor and process until smooth.

3 Pour the spicy mixture over the chicken. Turn the chicken portions over so that they are well coated in the marinade.

4 Transfer the chicken portions to the refrigerator and leave to marinate for up to 24 hours.

5 Preheat the barbecue. Remove the chicken from the marinade and cook over medium–hot coals for 30 minutes, turning the chicken over and basting occasionally with any remaining marinade, or until the chicken is browned and cooked through.

6 Transfer the chicken portions to individual serving plates and serve immediately.

NUTRITION		
Calories 158		Sugars 0.4g
Protein 29g		Fat 4g
Carbohydrate 2g		Saturates 1g

lemon grass skewers

serves four

2 long or 4 short lemon grass stalks

2 large boneless, skinless chicken
 breasts, roughly chopped

1 small egg white

1 carrot, finely grated

1 small fresh red chilli, deseeded
 and chopped

2 tbsp fresh garlic chives, chopped

2 tbsp chopped fresh coriander

salt and pepper

1 tbsp sunflower oil

TO GARNISH

fresh coriander sprigs

lime slices

NUTRITION

Calories 140	Sugars 2g
Protein 19g	Fat 7g
Carbohydrate 2g	Saturates 1g

COOK'S TIP

If you can't find lemon grass
stalks, use wooden or bamboo
skewers instead, and add
½ teaspoon ground lemon grass
with the other flavourings.

1 If the lemon grass stalks are long, cut them in half across the middle to make 4 short lengths. Cut each stalk in half lengthways, so you have 8 lemon grass sticks altogether.

2 Place the chicken pieces in a food processor with the egg white. Process to a smooth paste, then add the carrot, chilli, chives, coriander and salt and pepper. Process for a few seconds to mix well.

3 Leave the mixture to chill in the refrigerator for 15 minutes. Preheat the grill to medium. Divide the mixture into 8 equal-sized portions, and use your hands to shape the mixture around the lemon grass 'skewers'.

4 Brush the skewers with oil and grill under the hot grill for 4–6 minutes, turning them occasionally, or until golden brown and thoroughly cooked. Alternatively, barbecue over medium–hot coals.

5 Garnish with coriander sprigs and lime slices and serve hot.

citrus duckling skewers

serves twelve

3 skinless, boneless duckling breasts

1 small red onion, cut into wedges

1 small aubergine, cut into cubes

MARINADE

grated rind and juice of 1 lemon

grated rind and juice of 1 lime

grated rind and juice of 1 orange

1 garlic clove, crushed

1 tsp dried oregano

2 tbsp olive oil, plus extra for oiling

dash of Tabasco sauce

COOK'S TIP

For more zing add 1 teaspoon of chilli sauce to the marinade. The meat can be marinated for several hours, but it is best to marinate the vegetables separately for only 30 minutes.

1 Cut the duckling into bite-sized pieces. Place in a non-metallic bowl with the prepared vegetables.

2 To make the marinade, place the lemon, lime and orange rinds and juices, garlic, oregano, oil and Tabasco sauce in a screw-top jar and shake until well combined. Pour the marinade over the duckling and vegetables and toss to coat. Leave to marinate in the refrigerator for 30 minutes.

3 Preheat the barbecue. Remove the duck and vegetables from the marinade and thread them onto presoaked wooden skewers, reserving the marinade.

4 Barbecue the skewers on an oiled rack over medium–hot coals, turning and basting frequently with the reserved marinade, for 15–20 minutes until the meat is cooked through. Alternatively, cook under a preheated grill. Serve immediately.

NUTRITION	
Calories 205	Sugars 5g
Protein 24g	Fat 10g
Carbohydrate 5g	Saturates 2g

duck with berry sauce

450 g/1 lb boneless duck breasts

2 tbsp raspberry vinegar

2 tbsp brandy

1 tbsp clear honey

salt and pepper

1 tsp sunflower oil, for brushing

SAUCE

225 g/8 oz raspberries, thawed
   if frozen

300 ml/10 fl oz rosé wine

2 tsp cornflour blended with 4 tsp
   cold water

TO SERVE

2 kiwi fruit, peeled and thinly sliced

assorted vegetables

1 Skin and trim the duck breasts to remove any excess fat. Using a sharp knife, score the flesh in diagonal lines and pound it with a meat mallet or a covered rolling pin until it is 2 cm/¾ inch thick.

2 Place the duck breasts in a shallow dish. Mix the vinegar, brandy and honey together in a small bowl and spoon it over the duck. Cover and leave to chill in the refrigerator for 1 hour.

3 Preheat the grill. Drain the duck breasts, reserving the marinade, and place on the grill rack. Season and brush with a little oil. Cook for 10 minutes under the hot grill, turn over, season and brush with oil again. Cook for a further 8–10 minutes, or until the meat is cooked through.

NUTRITION	
Calories 293	Sugars 10g
Protein 28g	Fat 8g
Carbohydrate 13g	Saturates 2g

4 Meanwhile, make the sauce. Reserve about 55 g/2 oz raspberries and place the rest in a saucepan. Add the reserved marinade and the wine. Bring to the boil and simmer for 5 minutes, or until slightly reduced. Sieve the sauce into a bowl, pressing the raspberries with the back of a spoon. Return the liquid to the saucepan and add the cornflour paste. Heat through, stirring, or until thickened. Add the reserved raspberries and season to taste with salt and pepper.

5 Thinly slice the duck breasts and alternate with slices of kiwi fruit. on warmed serving plates. Spoon over the sauce and serve with vegetables.

turkey with cheese pockets

serves four

4 turkey breast pieces, about
  225 g/8 oz each

salt and pepper

4 portions full-fat cheese (such as
  Bel Paese), 15 g/½ oz each

4 sage leaves or ½ tsp dried sage

8 rashers rindless streaky bacon

4 tbsp olive oil

2 tbsp lemon juice

TO SERVE

salad leaves

cherry tomatoes

NUTRITION

Calories 518	Sugars 0g
Protein 66g	Fat 28g
Carbohydrate 0g	Saturates 9g

VARIATION

You can vary the cheese you use
to stuff the turkey – try grated
mozzarella or slices of Brie or
Camembert. Also try 1 teaspoon
of redcurrant jelly or cranberry
sauce in each pocket instead of
the sage.

1 Preheat the barbecue. Carefully
cut a pocket into the side of each
turkey breast. Open out each breast a
little and season inside with salt
and pepper.

2 Place a portion of cheese into
each pocket. Tuck a sage leaf into
each pocket, or sprinkle with a little
dried sage.

3 Stretch the bacon out with the
back of a knife. Wrap 2 pieces
around each turkey breast, covering
the pocket.

4 Mix the oil and lemon juice
together in a small bowl.

5 Barbecue the turkey over
medium–hot coals, 10 minutes
on each side, basting frequently with
the lemon mixture.

6 Transfer the turkey to warmed
serving plates. Serve with salad
leaves and cherry tomatoes.

Fish & Seafood

This selection of recipes exploits the contrasting characteristics of different fish and shellfish to the full. Fish that come in handy single-portion size are cooked whole for maximum succulence as well as ease of preparation, either with sealed-in seasonings in foil parcels, such as Lemon Herrings (see page 150), or directly on the barbecue rack in the case of Mackerel with Lime & Coriander (see page 154). The firm texture of tuna, swordfish and halibut, on the other hand, makes them ideally suited to the speedy searing of steaks in a ridged griddle pan. Prawns are also given the fast-food treatment, either stir-fried in Giant Garlic Prawns (see page 172) or deep-fried after initial marinating for enhanced flavour in Spicy Salt & Pepper Prawns (see page 169).

Lively, exotic flavourings abound in this chapter, from Mussels with Lemon Grass (see page 173) to Indonesian-style Spicy Cod (see page 179).

lemon herrings

serves four

4 herrings, gutted and scaled

4 bay leaves

salt

1 lemon, sliced

4 tbsp unsalted butter

2 tbsp chopped fresh parsley

½ tsp lemon pepper

NUTRITION

Calories 355		Sugars 0g
Protein 19g		Fat 31g
Carbohydrate 0g		Saturates 13g

1 Preheat the barbecue. Season the prepared herrings inside and out with salt to taste.

2 Place a bay leaf inside the cavity of each fish.

3 Place 4 squares of foil on the work surface and divide the lemon slices evenly between them. Place a fish on top of the lemon slices on each of the foil squares.

4 Beat the butter until softened, then mix in the parsley and lemon pepper. Dot the flavoured butter liberally all over the fish.

5 Wrap the fish tightly in the foil and barbecue over medium–hot coals for 15–20 minutes, or until the fish is cooked through – the flesh should be white in colour and firm to the touch (unwrap the foil to check, then rewrap).

6 Transfer the wrapped fish parcels to warmed serving plates.

7 Unwrap the foil parcels just before serving, but serve the fish in their cooking juices still in the parcels.

blackened fish

serves four

4 white fish steaks

1 tbsp paprika

1 tsp dried thyme

1 tsp cayenne pepper

1 tsp black pepper

½ tsp white pepper

½ tsp salt

¼ tsp ground allspice

50 g/1¾ oz unsalted butter

3 tbsp sunflower oil

mixed salad leaves, to serve

NUTRITION

Calories 331	Sugars 0g
Protein 37g	Fat 20g
Carbohydrate 0g	Saturates 8g

COOK'S TIP

A whole fish – red mullet, for example – rather than steaks is also delicious cooked this way. The spicy seasoning can also be used to coat chicken portions, if you prefer.

1 Preheat the barbecue. Rinse the fish under cold running water and pat dry with kitchen paper.

2 Mix the paprika, thyme, cayenne, black and white peppers, salt and allspice together in a shallow dish.

3 Place the butter and oil in a small saucepan and heat over a low heat, stirring occasionally, or until the butter melts.

4 Brush the butter mixture liberally all over the fish steaks on both sides.

5 Dip the fish into the spicy mix until well coated on both sides.

6 Barbecue the fish over hot coals for 10 minutes on each side, turning once. Continue to baste the fish with the remaining butter mixture during the cooking time. Transfer the fish to 4 large serving plates and serve with mixed salad leaves.

butterfly prawns

serves two–four

500 g/1 lb 2 oz or 16 raw tiger
   prawns, peeled, leaving
   tails intact
juice of 2 limes
1 tsp cardamom seeds
2 tsp cumin seeds, ground
2 tsp coriander seeds, ground
½ tsp ground cinnamon
1 tsp ground turmeric
1 garlic clove, crushed
1 tsp cayenne pepper
2 tbsp sunflower oil
cucumber slices, to garnish

NUTRITION	
Calories 183	Sugars 0g
Protein 28g	Fat 8g
Carbohydrate 0g	Saturates 1g

1 Soak 8 wooden skewers in a bowl of water for 20 minutes. Cut the prawns lengthways in half down to the tail and flatten out to form a symmetrical shape.

2 Thread a prawn onto 2 presoaked wooden skewers, with the tail between them, so that, when laid flat, the skewers hold the prawn in shape. Thread another 3 prawns onto these 2 skewers in the same way.

3 Repeat until you have 4 sets of 4 prawns each.

4 Lay the skewered prawns in a non-porous, non-metallic dish, and sprinkle over the lime juice.

5 Mix the spices and oil together, then coat the prawns well in the mixture. Cover the prawns and leave to chill for 4 hours.

6 Preheat the barbecue or grill. Cook over hot coals or place in a grill pan lined with foil and cook under the hot grill for 6 minutes, turning once.

7 Serve immediately, garnished with cucumber.

mackerel with lime & coriander

serves four

4 small mackerel, gutted

¼ tsp ground coriander

¼ tsp ground cumin

3 tbsp chopped fresh coriander

1 fresh red chilli, deseeded
   and chopped

grated rind and juice of 1 lime

2 tbsp sunflower oil

salt and pepper

salad leaves, to serve

TO GARNISH

fresh red chilli flowers (optional)

1 lime, sliced

NUTRITION

Calories 302	Sugars 0g
Protein 21g	Fat 24g
Carbohydrate 0g	Saturates 4g

1 Preheat the barbecue. Make the chilli flowers for the garnish (see Cook's Tip). Remove the heads from the prepared mackerel. Sprinkle the mackerel with the spices and season to taste with salt and pepper. Sprinkle 1 teaspoon of the chopped coriander inside the cavity of each fish.

2 Mix the remaining coriander, chilli, lime rind and juice and oil together in a small bowl. Brush the mixture liberally over the fish.

3 Cook the fish over hot coals for 3–4 minutes on each side, turning once. Brush frequently with the basting mixture. Transfer the fish to serving plates, garnish with chilli flowers, if using, and lime slices and serve with salad leaves.

COOK'S TIP

To make the chilli flowers, cut the tips of 8 small chillies lengthways into thin strips, leaving the chillies intact at the stem end. Remove the seeds and place the chillies in iced water until curled.

marinated fish

serves four

4 whole mackerel

4 tbsp chopped fresh marjoram

2 tbsp extra virgin olive oil

finely grated rind and juice of 1 lime

2 garlic cloves, crushed

salt and pepper

lime wedges, to garnish

green salad leaves, to serve

NUTRITION

Calories 361	Sugars 0g
Protein 26g	Fat 29g
Carbohydrate 0g	Saturates 5g

1 Using a sharp knife, clean, gut and scale the fish (see page 156), then cut 4 or 5 diagonal slashes on each side of the fish. Place the fish in a shallow non-metallic dish.

2 To make the marinade, mix the marjoram, oil, lime rind and juice, garlic and salt and pepper together.

3 Pour the mixture over the fish. Leave to marinate in the refrigerator for 30 minutes.

4 Preheat the grill, then cook the mackerel under the hot grill for 5–6 minutes on each side, brushing occasionally with the reserved marinade, or until golden.

5 Transfer the fish to serving plates. Pour over any remaining marinade, garnish with lime wedges and serve with salad leaves.

mediterranean sardines

serves four

8–12 fresh sardines

8–12 fresh thyme sprigs

3 tbsp lemon juice

4 tbsp olive oil

salt and pepper

TO SERVE

lemon wedges

tomato slices

mixed salad

NUTRITION

Calories 857		Sugars 0g
Protein 88g		Fat 56g
Carbohydrate 0g		Saturates 11g

VARIATION

For a slightly different flavour and texture, give the sardines a crispy coating by tossing them in dried breadcrumbs and basting them with a little olive oil.

1 Preheat the barbecue. Clean and gut the fish if this has not already been done by the fishmonger.

2 Remove the scales from the sardines by rubbing the back of a knife from tail to head along the body. Wash the sardines and pat dry with kitchen paper.

3 Tuck a fresh thyme sprig into the body of each sardine.

4 Transfer the sardines to a large non-metallic dish and season to taste with salt and pepper.

5 Beat the lemon juice and oil together in a bowl and pour the mixture over the sardines. Leave to marinate in the refrigerator for 30 minutes.

6 Remove the sardines from the marinade and place them in a hinged basket, if you have one, or on a rack. Barbecue the sardines over hot coals for 3–4 minutes on each side, basting frequently with any remaining marinade.

7 Serve the cooked sardines garnished with lemon wedges, tomato slices and a mixed salad.

tuna with anchovy butter

4 thick tuna steaks, about 225 g/
    8 oz each, and 2 cm/¾ inch thick
olive oil
ANCHOVY BUTTER
8 anchovy fillets in oil, drained
4 spring onions, finely chopped
1 tbsp finely grated orange rind
115 g/4 oz unsalted butter
¼ tsp lemon juice
salt and pepper
TO GARNISH
fresh flat-leaf parsley sprigs
orange rind strips

NUTRITION

Calories 564	Sugars 0g
Protein 55g	Fat 38g
Carbohydrate 0g	Saturates 19g

VARIATION

If you like your food particularly
hot and spicy, add a pinch of
dried chilli flakes to the anchovy
butter mixture for a little
extra punch.

1 Preheat the barbecue. To make the anchovy butter, very finely chop the anchovies and place them in a bowl with the spring onions, orange rind and softened butter. Beat until all of the ingredients are blended well together, seasoning to taste with lemon juice and pepper.

2 Place the flavoured butter on a sheet of baking paper and roll up into a log shape. Fold over the ends and place in the freezer for 15 minutes to become firm.

3 Cook the tuna steaks for 2 minutes on an oiled barbecue rack over hot coals. Alternatively, cook in an oiled, ridged griddle pan over a high heat, in batches if necessary. Turn the steaks over and cook for 2 minutes for rare, or up to 4 minutes for well done. Season to taste with salt and pepper.

4 Transfer the tuna steaks to warmed serving plates and place 2 thin slices of anchovy butter on each steak. Garnish with parsley sprigs and strips of orange rind and serve.

skate with black butter

serves four

900 g/2 lb skate wings, cut into 4

175 g/6 oz butter

50 ml/2 fl oz red wine vinegar

15 g/½ oz capers, drained

1 tbsp chopped fresh parsley

salt and pepper

COURT-BOUILLON

850 ml/1½ pints cold water

850 ml/1½ pints dry white wine

3 tbsp white wine vinegar

2 large carrots, roughly chopped

1 onion, roughly chopped

2 celery sticks, roughly chopped

2 leeks, roughly chopped

2 garlic cloves, roughly chopped

2 fresh bay leaves

4 fresh parsley sprigs

4 fresh thyme sprigs

6 black peppercorns

1 tsp salt

green vegetables, to serve

NUTRITION

Calories 381	Sugars 0g
Protein 34g	Fat 27g
Carbohydrate 0g	Saturates 17g

1 Begin by making the court-bouillon. Place all of the ingredients in a large saucepan and bring slowly to the boil. Cover and simmer gently for 30 minutes. Sieve the liquid through a fine sieve into a clean saucepan. Return to the boil and simmer fast, uncovered, for 15–20 minutes, or until reduced to 600 ml/1 pint.

2 Place the skate in a wide shallow pan and pour the court-bouillon over it. Bring to the boil and simmer very gently for 15 minutes, or a little longer, depending on the thickness of the skate. Drain the fish and put to one side, keeping it warm.

3 Meanwhile, melt the butter in a frying pan. Cook over a medium heat until the butter changes colour to a dark brown and smells very nutty.

4 Add the vinegar, capers and parsley and simmer for 1 minute. Season to taste with salt and pepper. Pour over the fish. Serve seasonal fresh green vegetables of your choice.

smoky fish skewers

serves four

350 g/12 oz smoked cod fillet

350 g/12 oz cod fillet

8 large raw prawns

8 bay leaves

fresh dill sprigs, to garnish (optional)

MARINADE

4 tbsp sunflower oil, plus extra
    for brushing

2 tbsp lemon or lime juice

grated rind of ½ lemon or lime

¼ tsp dried dill

salt and pepper

NUTRITION

Calories 221	Sugars 0g
Protein 33g	Fat 10g
Carbohydrate 0g	Saturates 1g

1 Skin both types of cod and cut the flesh into bite-sized pieces. Peel the prawns, leaving the tails intact.

2 To make the marinade, mix the oil, lemon juice and rind, dried dill and salt and pepper together in a shallow non-metallic dish.

3 Place the prepared fish in the marinade and stir well until the fish is coated on all sides. Cover and leave to marinate in the refrigerator for 30 minutes.

4 Preheat the barbecue. Thread the fish onto 4 metal skewers, alternating the fish with the prawns and bay leaves.

COOK'S TIP

Cod fillet can be rather flaky, so choose the thicker end, which is easier to cut into chunky pieces. Cook the fish on foil rather than directly on the rack, so that if the fish breaks away from the skewer it is not wasted.

5 Cover the barbecue rack with lightly oiled foil. Place the fish skewers on top and cook over hot coals for 5–10 minutes, basting with any remaining marinade. Turn once.

6 Transfer the skewers to a warmed serving plate, garnish with fresh dill sprigs, if using, and serve.

stuffed monkfish tail

serves six

750 g/1 lb 10 oz monkfish tail,
   skinned and trimmed

6 slices Parma ham

4 tbsp chopped fresh mixed herbs such
   as parsley, chives, basil and sage

1 tsp finely grated lemon rind

salt and pepper

2 tbsp olive oil

shredded stir-fried vegetables,
   to serve

NUTRITION

Calories 154	Sugars 0g
Protein 24g	Fat 6g
Carbohydrate 0g	Saturates 1g

1 Preheat the oven to 200°C/400°F/ Gas Mark 6. Using a sharp knife, carefully cut down each side of the central bone of the monkfish to leave 2 fillets. Rinse the fillets under cold running water and pat dry with kitchen paper.

2 Lay the Parma ham slices widthways on a work surface so that they overlap slightly. Lay the fish fillets lengthways on top of the ham so that the 2 cut sides face each other.

3 Mix the chopped herbs and lemon rind together. Season well with salt and pepper. Pack this mixture onto the cut surface of 1 monkfish fillet. Press the 2 fillets together and wrap tightly with the Parma ham slices. Secure with string or cocktail sticks.

4 Heat the oil in a large frying pan over a low heat. Place the fish in the frying pan, seam-side down first, and brown the wrapped fish all over.

5 Transfer the fish to a large ovenproof dish and cook in the preheated oven for 25 minutes until golden and the fish is tender. Remove from the oven and leave to rest for 10 minutes before slicing thickly. Serve with shredded stir-fried vegetables.

szechuan white fish

serves four

1 small egg, beaten

3 tbsp plain flour

4 tbsp dry white wine

3 tbsp light soy sauce

350 g/12 oz white fish fillets, cut
into 4-cm/1½-inch cubes

vegetable oil, for frying

1 garlic clove, cut into slivers

1 tsp finely chopped fresh
root ginger

1 onion, finely chopped

1 celery stick, chopped

1 fresh red chilli, chopped

3 spring onions, chopped

1 tsp rice wine vinegar

½ tsp ground Szechuan pepper

175 ml/6 fl oz fish stock

1 tsp caster sugar

1 tsp cornflour

2 tsp water

NUTRITION

Calories 225	Sugars 3g
Protein 20g	Fat 8g
Carbohydrate 17g	Saturates 1g

1 Beat the egg, flour, wine and 1 tablespoon of the soy sauce together to make a batter. Dip the fish into the batter to coat well.

2 Heat the oil in a preheated wok or large heavy-based frying pan. Reduce the heat slightly, add the fish in batches and cook for 2–3 minutes, or until golden brown. Remove the fish with a slotted spoon, drain on kitchen paper and keep warm.

3 Pour all but 1 tablespoon of the oil from the wok and return it to the heat. Add the garlic, ginger, onion, celery, chilli and spring onions and stir-fry for 1–2 minutes. Stir in the remaining soy sauce and the vinegar.

4 Add the Szechuan pepper, stock and caster sugar to the wok. Mix the cornflour with the water to form a smooth paste and stir it into the stock. Bring to the boil and cook, stirring, for 1 minute, or until the sauce thickens and clears.

5 Return the fish to the wok and cook for 1–2 minutes. Serve immediately.

thai-spiced salmon

2.5-cm/1-inch piece fresh root
    ginger, grated

1 tsp coriander seeds, crushed

½ tsp chilli powder

1 tbsp lime juice

1 tsp sesame oil

4 pieces salmon fillet with skin,
    about 150 g/5½ oz each

2 tbsp vegetable oil

stir-fried vegetables, to serve

NUTRITION	
Calories 329	Sugars 0.1g
Protein 30g	Fat 23g
Carbohydrate 0.1g	Saturates 4g

COOK'S TIP

Use a heavy-based frying pan or griddle for this recipe, so the fish cooks evenly throughout without sticking. If it is very thick, turn it over carefully to cook on the other side for 2–3 minutes.

1 Mix the ginger, crushed coriander, chilli powder, lime juice and sesame oil together.

2 Place the salmon on a wide non-metallic plate or dish and spoon the mixture over the flesh side of the fillets, spreading it to coat each piece of salmon evenly.

3 Cover the dish and chill in the refrigerator for 30 minutes.

4 Heat a wide heavy-based frying pan or griddle pan with the oil over a high heat. Place the salmon on the hot pan or griddle, skin-side down.

5 Cook the salmon for 4–5 minutes, without turning, or until the salmon is crusty underneath and the flesh flakes easily. Serve immediately with stir-fried vegetables.

baked sea bass

serves four

2 sea bass, about 1 kg/2 lb 4 oz
   each, gutted and scaled

2 spring onions, green part only,
   cut into strips

5-cm/2-inch piece fresh root ginger,
   cut into strips

2 garlic cloves, unpeeled and
   lightly crushed

2 tbsp mirin or dry sherry

salt and pepper

TO SERVE

pickled sushi ginger (optional)

soy sauce

NUTRITION

Calories 140	Sugars 0.1g
Protein 29g	Fat 1g
Carbohydrate 0.1g	Saturates 0.2g

1 Preheat the barbecue. For each fish, lay out a double thickness of foil and oil the top piece well or lay a piece of baking paper over the foil.

2 Place the fish in the middle of the foil and expose the cavities. Divide the spring onion, ginger and garlic between each cavity.

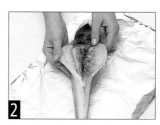

3 Pour the mirin over the fish and season to taste with salt and pepper.

4 Close the cavities and lay each fish on its side. Fold over the foil to encase the fish and seal the edges securely. Fold each end neatly.

5 Cook over medium–hot coals for 15 minutes, turning once.

6 To serve, remove the foil and cut each fish into 2–3 pieces. Serve with the pickled sushi ginger, if using, accompanied by soy sauce.

COOK'S TIP

Fresh sea bass is just as delicious when cooked very simply. Stuff the fish with garlic and chopped herbs, brush with olive oil and bake in the oven.

salmon fillet with herbs

serves four

½ large bunch dried thyme

5 fresh rosemary branches,
    15–20 cm/6–8 inches long

8 bay leaves

1 kg/2 lb 4 oz salmon fillet

1 fennel bulb, cut into 8 pieces

2 tbsp lemon juice

2 tbsp olive oil

fresh salad leaves, to serve

NUTRITION	
Calories 507	Sugars 0.4g
Protein 46g	Fat 35g
Carbohydrate 0.5g	Saturates 6g

1 Preheat the barbecue. Make a base on the hot barbecue with the thyme, rosemary and bay leaves, overlapping them so that they cover a slightly larger area than the salmon.

2 Carefully place the salmon on top of the herbs.

VARIATION

Use whatever combination of herbs you may have to hand – but avoid the stronger tasting herbs, such as sage and marjoram, which are unsuitable for fish.

3 Arrange the fennel around the edge of the fish.

4 Mix the lemon juice and oil together, then brush the salmon with it. Cover the salmon loosely with a piece of foil, to keep it moist.

5 Cook over hot coals for 20–30 minutes, basting frequently with the lemon mixture.

6 Remove the cooked salmon from the barbecue, cut it into slices, and arrange the fennel around it. Serve with salad leaves.

noisettes of salmon

serves four

4 salmon steaks

50 g/1¾ oz butter, softened

1 garlic clove, crushed

2 tsp mustard seeds

2 tbsp chopped fresh thyme

1 tbsp chopped fresh parsley

salt and pepper

2 tbsp vegetable oil

4 tomatoes, peeled, deseeded
    and chopped

green vegetables or salad,
    to serve

NUTRITION

Calories 381	Sugars 3g	
Protein 36g	Fat 26g	
Carbohydrate 3g	Saturates 4g	

COOK'S TIP

You can make cod steaks into
noisettes in the same way. Cook
them with butter flavoured with
chives and basil.

1 Preheat the oven to 200°C/400°F/
Gas Mark 6. Carefully remove the
central bone from the salmon steaks
and cut them in half. Curl each piece
around to form a medallion and tie
with string. Blend the butter, garlic,
mustard seeds, thyme, parsley and salt
and pepper together and reserve.

2 Heat the oil in a preheated ridged
griddle pan or large frying pan
over a medium heat. Add the salmon
noisettes and brown on both sides, in
batches if necessary. Drain on kitchen
paper and leave to cool.

3 Cut 4 pieces of baking paper into
30-cm/12-inch squares. Place
2 salmon noisettes on top of each
square and top with a little of the
flavoured butter and chopped tomato.
Draw up the edges of the paper and
fold together to enclose the fish. Place
on a baking sheet.

4 Cook in the preheated oven
for 10–15 minutes, or until the
salmon is cooked through. Serve while
still warm with green vegetables or
salad of your choice.

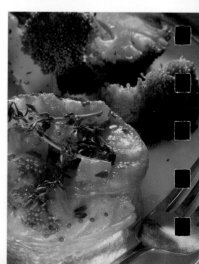

spicy salt & pepper prawns

serves four

250–300 g/9–10½ oz raw prawns
in their shells, thawed if frozen

1 tbsp light soy sauce

1 tsp rice wine or dry sherry

2 tsp cornflour

vegetable oil, for deep-frying

2–3 spring onions, to garnish

SPICY SALT & PEPPER

1 tbsp salt

1 tsp ground Szechuan peppercorns

1 tsp Chinese five-spice powder

NUTRITION

Calories 160		Sugars 0.2g	
Protein 17g		Fat 10g	
Carbohydrate 0.5g		Saturates 1g	

1 Pull the soft legs off the prawns, but keep the body shell on. Dry well on kitchen paper.

2 Place the prawns in a bowl with the soy sauce, rice wine and cornflour. Turn the prawns to coat thoroughly in the mixture and leave to marinate in the refrigerator for 25–30 minutes.

3 To make the Spicy Salt & Pepper, mix the salt, ground Szechuan peppercorns and five-spice powder together. Place in a dry frying pan and stir-fry for 3–4 minutes over a low heat, stirring constantly to prevent the spices burning on the base of the frying pan. Remove from the heat and leave to cool.

4 Heat the oil in a preheated wok or large frying pan until smoking. Add the prawns, in batches, and deep-fry until golden brown. Remove the prawns from the wok with a slotted spoon and drain on kitchen paper.

5 Place the spring onions in a bowl, pour over 1 tablespoon of the hot oil and leave for 30 seconds. Serve the prawns garnished with the spring onions, and with the Spicy Salt & Pepper as a dip.

fish with yucatan flavours

serves eight

4 tbsp annatto seeds, soaked in
　　water overnight
3 garlic cloves, finely chopped
1 tbsp mild chilli powder
1 tbsp paprika
1 tsp ground cumin
½ tsp dried oregano
2 tbsp beer or tequila
juice of 1 lime and 1 orange or
　　3 tbsp pineapple juice
2 tbsp olive oil
2 tbsp chopped fresh coriander
¼ tsp ground cinnamon
¼ tsp ground cloves
1 kg/2 lb 4 oz swordfish steaks
banana leaves, for wrapping
　　(optional)
fresh coriander sprigs, to garnish
orange wedges, to serve

NUTRITION	
Calories 179	Sugars 1g
Protein 24g	Fat 8g
Carbohydrate 1g	Saturates 2g

1 Drain the annatto, then crush them to a paste with a pestle and mortar. Work in the garlic, chilli powder, paprika, cumin, oregano, beer, fruit juice, oil, coriander, cinnamon and cloves.

2 Smear the paste over the fish, cover and leave to marinate in the refrigerator for at least 3 hours or overnight.

3 Preheat the barbecue or grill. Wrap the fish steaks in banana leaves, tying with string to make parcels. Bring enough water to the boil in a steamer, then add a batch of parcels to the top part of the steamer and steam for 15 minutes, or until the fish is cooked through.

4 Alternatively, cook the fish without wrapping in the banana leaves. To cook on the barbecue, place in a hinged basket or on a rack and cook over hot coals for 5–6 minutes on each side, or until cooked through. Alternatively, cook the fish under the hot grill for 5–6 minutes on each side, or until cooked through.

5 Garnish with coriander sprigs and serve with orange wedges for squeezing over the fish.

giant garlic prawns

125 ml/4 fl oz olive oil

4 garlic cloves, finely chopped

2 hot fresh red chillies, deseeded
   and finely chopped

450 g/1 lb cooked king prawns

2 tbsp chopped fresh
   flat-leaf parsley

salt and pepper

lemon wedges, to garnish

NUTRITION	
Calories 385	Sugars 0g
Protein 26g	Fat 31g
Carbohydrate 1g	Saturates 5g

COOK'S TIP

If you can get hold of raw
prawns, cook them as above but
increase the cooking time to 5–6
minutes until the prawns are
cooked through and turn bright
pink. If you are using frozen
prawns, make sure they are
thoroughly thawed before
cooking.

1 Heat the oil in a large heavy-based frying pan over a low heat. Add the garlic and chillies and cook, stirring occasionally, for 1–2 minutes, or until softened, but not coloured.

2 Add the prawns and stir-fry for 2–3 minutes, or until heated through and coated in the oil and garlic mixture.

3 Turn off the heat and add the chopped parsley, stirring well to mix. Season to taste with salt and pepper.

4 Divide the prawns and garlic-flavoured oil between warmed serving dishes and garnish with lemon wedges and serve.

mussels with lemon grass

serves four

750 g/1 lb 10 oz live mussels

1 tbsp sesame oil

3 shallots, finely chopped

2 garlic cloves, finely chopped

1 stalk lemon grass

2 kaffir lime leaves

2 tbsp chopped fresh coriander

finely grated rind of 1 lime

2 tbsp lime juice

300 ml/10 fl oz hot vegetable stock

fresh coriander, to garnish

NUTRITION

Calories 194	Sugars 0g
Protein 33g	Fat 7g
Carbohydrate 1g	Saturates 1g

COOK'S TIP

Mussels are now farmed, so they should be available from good fishmongers throughout the year.

1 Clean the mussels thoroughly by scrubbing or scraping the shells and pulling out any beards that are attached to them. Discard any with broken shells or any that refuse to close when tapped.

2 Heat the oil in a large saucepan. Add the shallots and garlic and fry gently until softened, about 2 minutes.

3 Bruise the lemon grass, using a meat mallet or rolling pin, and add to the pan with the kaffir lime leaves, coriander, lime rind and juice, mussels and stock. Cook, covered, over a high heat for 3–4 minutes, shaking the saucepan occasionally, or until the mussels have opened.

4 Lift the mussels out into 4 warmed soup plates, discarding any that remain closed. Boil the remaining liquid rapidly to reduce slightly. Remove the lemon grass and lime leaves, then pour the liquid over the mussels. Garnish with coriander and serve.

thai steamed mussels

serves two

1 kg/2 lb 4 oz live mussels in shells

2 shallots, finely chopped

1 lemon grass stalk, finely sliced

1 garlic clove, finely chopped

3 tbsp rice wine or dry sherry

2 tbsp lime juice

1 tbsp Thai fish sauce

4 tbsp chopped fresh basil

salt and pepper

25 g/1 oz butter

fresh basil leaves, to garnish

NUTRITION

Calories 252	Sugars 2g
Protein 22g	Fat 14g
Carbohydrate 8g	Saturates 8g

COOK'S TIP

If you prefer to serve this dish as a starter, this amount will be enough for four portions. Fresh clams in shells are also very good when cooked by this method.

1 Clean the mussels thoroughly by scrubbing or scraping the shells and pulling out any beards that are attached to them. Discard any with broken shells or any that refuse to close when tapped.

2 Place the shallots, lemon grass, garlic, rice wine, lime juice and fish sauce in a large heavy-based saucepan and place over a high heat.

3 Add the mussels, then cover and steam for 3–4 minutes, shaking the saucepan occasionally, or until the mussels have opened.

4 Discard any mussels that remain closed, then stir in the chopped basil and season to taste with salt and pepper.

5 Scoop out the mussels with a slotted spoon and divide between 2 deep bowls. Quickly whisk the butter into the pan juices, then pour the juices over the mussels.

6 Garnish each bowl with fresh basil leaves and serve.

red curry fish cakes

serves six

1 kg/2 lb 4 oz fish fillets or prepared
seafood, such as cod, haddock,
prawns, crabmeat or lobster

1 egg, beaten

2 tbsp chopped fresh coriander

1 tsp Thai red curry paste

1 bunch spring onions,
finely chopped

vegetable oil, for deep-frying

fresh red chilli flowers, to garnish
(see page 154)

CUCUMBER SALAD

1 large cucumber, peeled
and grated

2 shallots, grated

2 fresh red chillies, deseeded and
very finely chopped

2 tbsp Thai fish sauce

2 tbsp dried powdered shrimp

1½–2 tbsp lime juice

NUTRITION

Calories 203	Sugars 1g
Protein 32g	Fat 8g
Carbohydrate 1g	Saturates 1g

1 Place the fish in a food processor or blender with the egg, coriander and curry paste and process until smooth and well blended.

2 Transfer the mixture to a bowl, add the spring onions and mix well to combine.

3 Taking 2 tablespoons of the fish mixture at a time, shape into balls, then flatten them slightly with your fingers to make fish cakes.

4 Heat the oil in a preheated wok or frying pan until hot.

5 Add a few fish cakes to the wok and deep-fry for a few minutes until brown and cooked. Remove and drain on kitchen paper. Keep warm while cooking the remaining fish cakes.

6 To make the salad, mix the cucumber, shallots, chillies, fish sauce, dried shrimp and lime juice together. Garnish the salad with a chilli flower and serve with the fish cakes.

gingered monkfish

serves four

450 g/1 lb monkfish

1 tbsp grated fresh root ginger

2 tbsp sweet chilli sauce

1 tbsp corn oil

100 g/3½ oz fine asparagus

3 spring onions, diagonally sliced

1 tsp sesame oil

NUTRITION

Calories 133	Sugars 0g
Protein 21g	Fat 5g
Carbohydrate 1g	Saturates 1g

1 Cut the monkfish into bite-sized pieces. Mix the ginger and sweet chilli sauce together in a small bowl until thoroughly blended. Brush the ginger and chilli sauce mixture over the monkfish pieces, using a pastry brush.

2 Heat the corn oil in a preheated wok or large heavy-based frying pan.

3 Add the monkfish, asparagus and spring onions to the wok and stir-fry for 5 minutes, stirring gently so the fish and asparagus do not break up.

4 Remove the wok from the heat, drizzle the sesame oil over the stir-fry and toss well to combine.

5 Transfer the monkfish to warmed serving plates and serve immediately.

COOK'S TIP

Monkfish is quite expensive, but it is well worth using because it has a wonderful flavour and texture. You could use cubes of chunky cod fillet instead.

swordfish steaks

serves four

4 swordfish steaks, about
  150 g/5½ oz each
4 tbsp olive oil
1 garlic clove, crushed
1 tsp lemon rind
flat-leaf parsley sprigs, to garnish
SALSA VERDE
25 g/1 oz fresh flat-leaf parsley
15 g/½ oz mixed fresh herbs,
  such as basil, mint and chives
1 garlic clove, chopped
1 tbsp capers, drained and rinsed
1 tbsp green peppercorns in brine,
  drained
4 canned anchovy fillets in oil,
  drained and roughly chopped
1 tsp Dijon mustard
125 ml/4 fl oz extra virgin olive oil
salt and pepper

NUTRITION

Calories 548	Sugars 0g
Protein 28g	Fat 48g
Carbohydrate 1g	Saturates 7g

1 Rinse the swordfish steaks under cold running water and pat dry with kitchen paper. Arrange the steaks in a non-metallic dish. Mix the oil, garlic and lemon rind together in a small bowl and pour over the swordfish steaks. Cover and leave to marinate in the refrigerator for 1 hour.

2 To make the Salsa Verde, place the parsley, mixed herbs, garlic, capers, green peppercorns, anchovies, mustard and oil into a food processor or blender and process to a smooth paste, adding a little warm water if necessary. Season to taste with salt and pepper and reserve.

3 Remove the swordfish steaks from the marinade. Transfer to a preheated ridged griddle pan and cook for 2–3 minutes on each side until tender. Transfer the fish to 4 large serving plates, garnish with parsley sprigs and serve immediately with the Salsa Verde.

COOK'S TIP
Firm-fleshed fish is ideal for this recipe. Try tuna or shark instead.

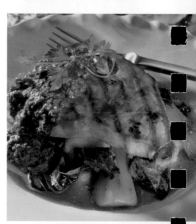

indonesian-style spicy cod

serves four

4 cod steaks

1 lemon grass stalk

1 small red onion, chopped

3 garlic cloves, chopped

2 fresh red chillies, deseeded
   and chopped

1 tsp grated fresh root ginger

¼ tsp ground turmeric

salt and pepper

2 tbsp butter, cut into small cubes

8 tbsp canned coconut milk

2 tbsp lemon juice

fresh red chillies, to garnish
   (optional)

mixed salad leaves, to serve

NUTRITION

Calories 146	Sugars 2g
Protein 19g	Fat 7g
Carbohydrate 2g	Saturates 4g

COOK'S TIP

If you prefer a milder flavour,
omit the chillies altogether. For a
hotter flavour, do not remove the
seeds from the chillies.

1 Preheat the barbecue. Rinse the cod steaks under cold running water and pat dry on kitchen paper.

2 Remove and discard the outer leaves from the lemon grass and thinly slice the inner section.

3 Place the lemon grass, onion, garlic, chillies, ginger and turmeric in a food processor and process until finely chopped. Season to taste with salt and pepper. Keeping the machine running, add the butter, coconut milk and lemon juice and process until well blended.

4 Place the fish in a shallow non-metallic dish. Pour over the coconut mixture and turn the fish until well coated.

5 If you have one, place the fish steaks in a hinged basket, which will make them easier to turn. Cook the fish steaks over hot coals for 15 minutes, or until the fish is cooked through, turning once. Transfer to 4 large serving plates, garnish with red chillies, if using, and serve with mixed salad leaves.

pan-seared halibut

serves four

1 tsp olive oil

4 halibut steaks, skinned, about
175 g/6 oz each

½ tsp cornflour mixed with 2 tsp
cold water

2 tbsp snipped fresh chives,
to garnish

RED ONION RELISH

2 red onions

6 shallots

1 tbsp lemon juice

2 tsp olive oil

2 tbsp red wine vinegar

2 tsp caster sugar

150 ml/5 fl oz fish stock

salt and pepper

COOK'S TIP

If raw onions make your eyes
water, try peeling them under
cold running water. Alternatively,
stand or sit well back from the
onion so that your face isn't
directly over it.

1 To make the relish, shred the
onions and shallots thinly, then
place in a small bowl and toss in the
lemon juice.

2 Heat the oil for the relish in a
frying pan over a medium heat.
Add the onions and shallots and fry
for 3–4 minutes, or until just softened.

3 Add the vinegar and sugar and
continue to cook for a further
2 minutes over a high heat. Pour in the
stock and season well with salt and
pepper. Bring to the boil and simmer
gently for a further 8–9 minutes, or
until the sauce has thickened and is
slightly reduced.

4 Brush a non-stick ridged griddle
pan or frying pan with oil and
heat over a medium–high heat until
hot. Press the fish into the pan to
seal, reduce the heat and cook for
4 minutes. Turn the fish over and
cook for 4–5 minutes, or until cooked
through. Drain on kitchen paper
and keep warm.

5 Stir the cornflour paste into the
onion relish and heat through,
stirring, or until thickened. Season to
taste with salt and pepper.

6 Pile the relish onto 4 warmed
serving plates and place a halibut
steak on top of each. Garnish with
snipped chives and serve.

NUTRITION	
Calories 197	Sugars 1g
Protein 31g	Fat 7g
Carbohydrate 2g	Saturates 1g

trout in red wine

serves four

4 fresh trout, about 300 g/
   10½ oz each

250 ml/9 fl oz red or white
   wine vinegar

300 ml/10 fl oz red or dry
   white wine

150 ml/5 fl oz water

1 carrot, sliced

2–4 bay leaves

thinly pared rind of 1 lemon

1 small onion, very thinly sliced

4 fresh parsley sprigs

4 fresh thyme sprigs

1 tsp black peppercorns

6–8 whole cloves

salt and pepper

85 g/3 oz butter

mixed salad, to serve

TO GARNISH

fresh parsley sprigs

lemon slices

NUTRITION

Calories 489	Sugars 0.6g
Protein 48g	Fat 27g
Carbohydrate 0.6g	Saturates 14g

1 Gut the trout, but leave their heads on. Dry on kitchen paper and lay the fish head to tail in a shallow container or baking tin large enough to hold them.

2 Bring the vinegar to the boil and pour slowly all over the fish. Leave the fish to marinate in the refrigerator for 20 minutes.

3 Meanwhile, place the wine, water, carrot, bay leaves, lemon rind, onion, herbs, peppercorns and cloves in a saucepan with a good pinch of salt and heat gently.

4 Drain the fish thoroughly, discarding the vinegar. Place the fish in a fish kettle or large frying pan so they touch. When the wine mixture boils, sieve gently over the fish so they are about half-covered. Cover and simmer very gently for 15 minutes.

5 Carefully remove the fish from the kettle, draining off and reserving as much of the liquid as possible. Arrange the fish in a serving dish and keep warm.

6 Boil the cooking liquid until reduced to 4–6 tablespoons. Melt the butter in a saucepan and sieve in the cooking liquor. Season and spoon over the fish. Garnish with parsley and lemon slices and serve with salad.

Vegetables

Vegetables are too good to be confined to a supporting role in your diet, especially in a low-carbohydrate eating plan. So here they take centre stage in a range of imaginative, flavourful main dishes. Enjoy the colourful medley of peppers, courgettes and baby aubergines, threaded onto skewers, in the recipe for Chargrilled Vegetables (see page 189), or savour the aromatic spices in the rich red Tomato Curry (see page 204).

In other recipes in this chapter, you will find vegetables perfectly partnered with a choice protein, such as vegetarian smoked tofu in Marinated Brochettes (see page 186) and fluffy eggs in Spinach & Herb Frittata (see page 211). You can even enjoy your vegetables with a limited amount of carbohydrates, with tender asparagus encased in crisp filo pastry and juicy mushrooms stuffed with a creamy potato filling.

marinated brochettes

serves four

1 lemon

1 garlic clove, crushed

4 tbsp olive oil

4 tbsp white wine vinegar

1 tbsp chopped fresh herbs, such as
  rosemary, parsley and thyme

salt and pepper

300 g/10½ oz smoked tofu, drained

350 g/12 oz mushrooms

fresh herbs, to garnish

TO SERVE

mixed salad leaves

cherry tomatoes, quartered

NUTRITION

Calories 192	Sugars 0.5g
Protein 11g	Fat 16g
Carbohydrate 1g	Saturates 2g

1 Finely grate the rind from the lemon and squeeze out the juice.

2 Add the garlic, oil, vinegar and chopped herbs and mix well. Season to taste with salt and pepper.

3 Slice the tofu into large chunks with a sharp knife. Thread the pieces onto presoaked wooden skewers, alternating them with the mushrooms.

4 Place the brochettes in a shallow non-metallic dish and pour over the marinade. Cover and leave to chill for 1–2 hours, turning the brochettes in the marinade occasionally.

5 Preheat the barbecue or grill. Remove the brochettes from the dish, reserving the marinade. Cook over medium–hot coals, brushing them frequently with the marinade and turning often, for 6 minutes, or until cooked through and golden brown. Alternatively, cook under the hot grill, turning frequently and brushing with the reserved marinade.

6 Transfer to warmed serving plates, garnish with fresh herbs and serve immediately with mixed salad leaves and cherry tomatoes.

braised tofu home-style

serves four

3 packets tofu, about 225 g/
    8 oz each (drained weight)
125 g/4½ oz boneless pork
1 leek
few small dried whole chillies,
    soaked
vegetable oil, for deep-frying
1–2 spring onions, cut into sections
2 tbsp crushed yellow bean sauce
1 tbsp light soy sauce
2 tsp rice wine or dry sherry
few drops sesame oil

NUTRITION	
Calories 218	Sugars 1g
Protein 17g	Fat 16g
Carbohydrate 2g	Saturates 2g

1 Split each packet of tofu into 3 slices crossways, then cut each slice diagonally into 2 triangles.

2 Cut the pork into small thin slices or shreds. Cut the leek into thin strips.

COOK'S TIP

Tofu is sold in three forms:
firm tofu, which can be
smoked, silken tofu or marinated
tofu. It is the solid kind that
is used for braising and stir-
frying. Silken tofu is usually
added to soups or sauces.

3 Drain the chillies, remove the seeds using the tip of a knife, then cut into small shreds.

4 Heat the oil in a preheated wok until smoking, then deep-fry the tofu triangles for 2–3 minutes, or until golden brown all over. Remove with a slotted spoon and drain on kitchen paper.

5 Pour off the hot oil, leaving about 1 tablespoon in the wok. Add the pork strips, spring onions and chillies and stir-fry for 1 minute, or until the pork changes colour.

6 Add the leek, tofu, yellow bean sauce, soy sauce and wine and braise for 2–3 minutes, stirring gently to blend well. Finally, sprinkle on the sesame oil and serve.

chargrilled vegetables

serves four

1 large red pepper

1 large green pepper

1 large orange pepper

1 large courgette

4 baby aubergines

2 red onions

2 tbsp lemon juice

1 tbsp olive oil

1 garlic clove, crushed

1 tbsp chopped fresh rosemary or
    1 tsp dried rosemary

salt and pepper

TO SERVE

cooked bulgar wheat

Fresh Tomato Relish (see page 103)

NUTRITION

Calories 66	Sugars 7g
Protein 2g	Fat 3g
Carbohydrate 7g	Saturates 0.5g

1 Preheat the barbecue or grill. Halve and deseed the peppers. Cut into pieces, 2.5 cm/1 inch wide.

2 Cut the courgettes in half lengthways and slice into 2.5-cm/1-inch pieces. Place the peppers and courgettes in a bowl.

3 Quarter the aubergines lengthways. Cut the onions into 8 even-sized wedges. Add the aubergines and onions to the peppers and courgettes.

4 Whisk the lemon juice, oil, garlic and rosemary together in a small bowl. Season to taste with salt and pepper. Pour the mixture over the vegetables and stir to coat them evenly.

5 Thread the vegetables onto 8 metal or presoaked wooden skewers. Cook over hot coals, turning frequently, for 8–10 minutes, or until softened and beginning to char. Alternatively, arrange the kebabs on the grill rack and cook under the hot grill, turning frequently, for 10–12 minutes, or until the vegetables are lightly charred and just softened.

6 Drain the vegetable kebabs and serve them immediately accompanied by Fresh Tomato Relish.

aubergine bake

serves four

3–4 tbsp olive oil

2 garlic cloves, crushed

2 large aubergines

100 g/3½ oz mozzarella cheese,
   thinly sliced

200 ml/7 fl oz passata

55 g/2 oz freshly grated
   Parmesan cheese

mixed salad leaves, to serve

NUTRITION	
Calories 232	Sugars 8g
Protein 10g	Fat 18g
Carbohydrate 8g	Saturates 6g

1 Preheat the oven to 200°C/400°F/ Gas Mark 6. Heat 2 tablespoons of the oil in a large heavy-based frying pan. Add the garlic and cook, stirring constantly, for 30 seconds.

2 Slice the aubergines lengthways. Add the slices to the frying pan and cook for 3–4 minutes on each side, or until tender. (You will probably have to cook them in batches, so add the remaining oil as necessary.)

3 Remove the aubergines and drain on kitchen paper.

4 Place a layer of aubergine in a shallow ovenproof dish. Cover with a layer of mozzarella, then pour over a third of the passata. Continue layering in the same order, finishing with a layer of passata on top.

5 Generously sprinkle the grated Parmesan cheese over the top and bake in the preheated oven for 25–30 minutes.

6 Transfer to serving plates and leave to cool, then serve warm or cold with salad leaves.

asparagus parcels

serves four

100 g/3½ oz fine tip asparagus

1 red pepper, deseeded and
thinly sliced

50 g/1¾ oz beansprouts

2 tbsp plum sauce

1 egg yolk

8 sheets filo pastry

sunflower oil, for deep-frying

chilli dipping sauce, to serve

NUTRITION

Calories 194	Sugars 2g
Protein 3g	Fat 16g
Carbohydrate 11g	Saturates 4g

1 Place the asparagus, pepper and beansprouts in a large bowl. Add the plum sauce to the vegetables and mix well.

2 Beat the egg yolk and reserve until required.

3 Lay the sheets of filo pastry out on a clean work surface, and cover with a damp cloth to prevent them drying out.

4 Working with one sheet of filo pastry at a time, place a small quantity of the asparagus and red pepper filling at the top end of the sheet. Brush all the edges of the filo pastry with a little of the beaten egg yolk. Roll up the sheet, tucking in the ends to enclose the filling like a spring roll. Continue filling and rolling the remaining filo pastry sheets.

5 Heat the oil for deep-frying in a preheated wok. Carefully cook the parcels, 2 at a time, in the hot oil for 4–5 minutes, or until crispy.

6 Remove the parcels with a slotted spoon and leave them to drain on kitchen paper. Transfer the parcels to warmed serving plates and serve immediately with a dipping sauce.

peppers with chestnuts

serves four

225 g/8 oz leeks

sunflower oil, for deep-frying

1 yellow pepper, deseeded
    and diced

1 green pepper, deseeded and diced

1 red pepper, deseeded and diced

200 g/7 oz canned water chestnuts,
    drained and sliced

2 garlic cloves, crushed

3 tbsp light soy sauce

NUTRITION

Calories 192		Sugars 5g	
Protein 3g		Fat 14g	
Carbohydrate 13g		Saturates 13g	

1 Thinly shred the leeks. Heat the oil for deep-frying in a preheated wok or large heavy-based saucepan.

2 Add the leeks to the wok and fry for 2–3 minutes, or until crispy. Remove with a slotted spoon and drain on kitchen paper. Reserve.

3 Pour all but 3 tablespoons of the oil from the wok. Add the yellow, green and red peppers and stir-fry over a high heat for 5 minutes, or until they begin to brown at the edges and have softened.

4 Add the water chestnuts, garlic and light soy sauce to the wok and stir-fry the vegetables for a further 2–3 minutes.

5 Spoon the stir-fry onto warmed serving plates, sprinkle with the reserved crispy leeks and serve.

mixed bean pan-fry

serves four

350 g/12 oz mixed green beans,
   such as French and broad beans
2 tbsp vegetable oil
2 garlic cloves, crushed
1 red onion, halved and sliced
225 g/8 oz marinated tofu pieces
   (drained weight)
1 tbsp lemon juice
½ tsp ground turmeric
1 tsp ground mixed spice
150 ml/5 fl oz vegetable stock
2 tsp sesame seeds

NUTRITION

Calories 179	Sugars 4g
Protein 10g	Fat 11g
Carbohydrate 10g	Saturates 1g

VARIATION

Add lime juice instead of lemon,
for an alternative citrus flavour.
Use smoked tofu instead of
marinated tofu, if you prefer.

1 Slice the French beans, then shell the broad beans and reserve until required.

2 Heat the oil in a large frying pan. Add the garlic and onion and sauté for 2 minutes, stirring well.

3 Add the tofu and cook for 2–3 minutes, or until just beginning to brown.

4 Add the reserved French beans and broad beans. Stir in the lemon juice, turmeric, mixed spice and stock and bring to the boil.

5 Reduce the heat and simmer for 5–7 minutes, or until the beans are tender. Sprinkle with sesame seeds and serve immediately.

vegetable stir-fry with eggs

serves four

2 eggs

225 g/8 oz carrots

350 g/12 oz white cabbage

2 tbsp vegetable oil

1 red pepper, deseeded and
   thinly sliced

150 g/5½ oz beansprouts

1 tbsp tomato ketchup

2 tbsp soy sauce

75 g/2¾ oz salted peanuts,
   chopped

peanut sauce, to serve

NUTRITION

Calories 269	Sugars 12g
Protein 12g	Fat 19g
Carbohydrate 14g	Saturates 3g

COOK'S TIP

The eggs are cooled in cold water after cooking in order to prevent the egg yolk turning black around the edges.

1 Bring a small saucepan of water to the boil. Add the eggs and cook for 7 minutes. Remove the eggs from the saucepan and cool under cold running water for 1 minute. Peel the eggs, then cut into quarters.

2 Roughly grate the carrots and finely shred the white cabbage. Heat the oil in a preheated wok or large heavy-based frying pan.

3 Add the carrots, cabbage and red pepper to the wok and stir-fry for 3 minutes.

4 Add the beansprouts to the wok and stir-fry for 2 minutes.

5 Mix the ketchup and soy sauce together in a small bowl and add to the wok, stirring well to combine.

6 Add the chopped peanuts to the wok and stir-fry for 1 minute.

7 Transfer the stir-fry to warmed serving plates and garnish with the hard-boiled egg quarters. Serve with a peanut sauce.

vegetable chop suey

serves four

1 yellow pepper, deseeded

1 red pepper, deseeded

1 carrot

1 courgette

1 fennel bulb

1 onion

55 g/2 oz mangetout

2 tbsp peanut oil

3 garlic cloves, crushed

1 tsp grated fresh root ginger

115 g/4 oz beansprouts

2 tsp light brown sugar

2 tbsp light soy sauce

125 ml/4 fl oz vegetable stock

NUTRITION

Calories 155	Sugars 6g
Protein 4g	Fat 12g
Carbohydrate 9g	Saturates 2g

1 Cut the peppers, carrot, courgette and fennel into thin slices. Cut the onion into quarters, then cut each quarter in half. Slice the mangetout diagonally to create the maximum surface area.

2 Heat the oil in a preheated wok. Add the garlic and ginger and stir-fry for 30 seconds. Add the onion and stir-fry for a further 30 seconds.

VARIATION
Use any combination of colourful vegetables that you have to hand to make this versatile dish.

3 Add the peppers, carrot, courgette, fennel and mangetout to the wok and stir-fry for 2 minutes.

4 Add the beansprouts to the wok and stir in the sugar, soy sauce and stock. Reduce the heat to low and simmer for 1–2 minutes, or until the vegetables are tender and coated in the sauce.

5 Transfer the vegetables and sauce to a serving dish and serve immediately.

dolmades

serves four

225 g/8 oz vine leaves preserved in
    brine, about 40 in total
150 ml/5 fl oz olive oil
4 tbsp lemon juice
300 ml/10 fl oz water
lemon wedges, to serve
FILLING
115 g/4 oz long-grain rice,
    not basmati
350 ml/12 fl oz water
salt and pepper
55 g/2 oz currants
55 g/2 oz pine kernels, chopped
2 spring onions, very finely chopped
1 tbsp very finely chopped
    fresh coriander
1 tbsp very finely chopped
    fresh parsley
1 tbsp very finely chopped fresh dill
finely grated rind of ½ lemon

NUTRITION

Calories 82	Sugars 2g
Protein 1g	Fat 7g
Carbohydrate 5g	Saturates 1g

1 Rinse the vine leaves in cold water and place them in a heatproof bowl. Cover with boiling water and soak for 5 minutes. Drain.

2 Place the rice and water in a saucepan. Add a pinch of salt and cook for 10–12 minutes, or until the liquid is absorbed. Drain and cool.

3 Stir the currants, pine kernels, spring onions, herbs and lemon rind into the rice. Season.

4 Line the base of a large frying pan with 3 or 4 of the thickest vine leaves or with any that are torn. Place a vine leaf on the work surface, vein-side upwards, with the pointed end facing away from you. Place a small, compact roll of the rice stuffing at the base of the leaf. Fold up the bottom end of the leaf.

5 Fold in each side of the leaf to overlap in the centre. Roll up the leaf around the filling and squeeze lightly in your hand to shape and seal it. Continue with the remaining vine leaves and stuffing mixture.

6 Place the rolls in a single layer in the frying pan, seam-side down. Combine the oil, lemon juice and water and pour into the frying pan.

7 Fit a heatproof plate over the rolls and cover the frying pan. Simmer for 30 minutes, then remove the frying pan from the heat and leave the stuffed vine leaves to cool in the liquid. Serve chilled with lemon wedges.

cantonese garden vegetables

serves four

2 tbsp groundnut oil

1 tsp Chinese five-spice powder

75 g/2¾ oz baby carrots, halved

2 celery sticks, sliced

2 baby leeks, sliced

50 g/1¾ oz mangetout

4 baby courgettes, halved
   lengthways

8 baby sweetcorn

225 g/8 oz marinated tofu pieces
   (drained weight)

4 tbsp fresh orange juice

1 tbsp clear honey

TO GARNISH

celery leaves

orange zest

NUTRITION

Calories 130	Sugars 8g
Protein 6g	Fat 8g
Carbohydrate 8g	Saturates 1g

1 Heat the oil in a preheated wok until almost smoking. Add the five-spice powder, carrots, celery, leeks, mangetout, courgettes and baby sweetcorn and stir-fry for 3–4 minutes.

2 Add the tofu and cook for a further 2 minutes, stirring.

3 Stir in the orange juice and honey, reduce the heat and stir-fry for 1–2 minutes.

4 Transfer the stir-fry to a serving dish, garnish with celery leaves and orange zest and serve immediately.

COOK'S TIP

Chinese five-spice powder is a mixture of fennel, star anise, cinnamon bark, cloves and Szechuan pepper. It is very pungent so should be used sparingly. If kept in an airtight container, it will keep indefinitely.

oven-baked risotto

serves four

4 tbsp olive oil

400 g/14 oz portobello or large field
  mushrooms, thickly sliced

115 g/4 oz pancetta or thick-cut
  smoked bacon, diced

1 large onion, finely chopped

2 garlic cloves, finely chopped

350 g/12 oz arborio or carnaroli rice

1.2 litres/2 pints chicken stock,
  simmering

2 tbsp chopped fresh tarragon or
  flat-leaf parsley

salt and pepper

85 g/3 oz freshly grated Parmesan
  cheese, plus extra for sprinkling

NUTRITION

Calories 428	Sugars 2g
Protein 15g	Fat 18g
Carbohydrate 14g	Saturates 6g

1 Preheat the oven to 180°C/
350°F/Gas Mark 4. Heat
2 tablespoons of the oil in a large
heavy-based frying pan over a
high heat. Add the mushrooms and
stir-fry for 2–3 minutes, or until golden
and tender-crisp. Transfer to a plate.

2 Add the pancetta to the frying
pan and cook for 2 minutes,
stirring frequently, or until crisp and
golden. Remove with a slotted spoon
and add to the mushrooms on
the plate.

3 Heat the remaining oil in a heavy-
based saucepan over a medium
heat. Add the onion and cook for
2 minutes. Add the garlic and rice and
cook, stirring, for 2 minutes, or until
the rice is well coated with the oil.

4 Gradually stir the stock into the
rice, then add the mushroom and
pancetta mixture and the tarragon.
Season to taste with salt and pepper.
Bring to the boil.

5 Remove the saucepan from the
heat and transfer to a casserole.

6 Cover and bake in the preheated
oven for 20 minutes, or until the
rice is almost tender and most of the
liquid has been absorbed. Uncover and
stir in the Parmesan cheese. Continue
to bake for 15 minutes longer, or until
the rice is tender but still firm to the
bite. Serve immediately with extra
Parmesan cheese for sprinkling.

baked aubergine gratin

serves four–six

1 large aubergine, about
800 g/1 lb 12 oz
300 g/10½ oz mozzarella cheese
85 g/3 oz Parmesan cheese
olive oil
about 250 ml/9 fl oz Tomato Sauce
(see page 74)
salt and pepper
shredded lettuce, to serve

NUTRITION

Calories 261	Sugars 5g
Protein 20g	Fat 18g
Carbohydrate 6g	Saturates 10g

1 Top and tail the aubergine and, using a sharp knife, cut it into 5-mm/¼-inch slices crossways. Arrange the slices on a large plate, sprinkle with salt and leave to drain for 30 minutes.

2 Preheat the oven to 200°C/400°F/Gas Mark 6. Drain and grate the mozzarella cheese and finely grate the Parmesan cheese.

3 Rinse the aubergine slices under cold running water and pat dry with kitchen paper. Lightly brush a baking sheet with oil and arrange the aubergine slices in a single layer. Brush the tops with oil.

4 Roast in the preheated oven for 5 minutes. Using tongs, turn the slices over, then brush with a little more oil and bake for a further 5 minutes, or until the aubergine is cooked through and tender. Do not turn off the oven.

5 Spread about 1 tablespoon oil over the base of a gratin dish or other ovenproof serving dish. Add a layer of aubergine slices, about a quarter of the Tomato Sauce and top with a quarter of the mozzarella. Season to taste with salt and pepper.

6 Continue layering until all the ingredients are used, ending with a layer of sauce. Sprinkle the Parmesan cheese over the top. Bake for 30 minutes, or until bubbling. Leave to stand for 5 minutes before serving with shredded lettuce.

tomato curry

serves four

400 g/14 oz canned tomatoes

1 tsp finely chopped fresh
    root ginger

1 tsp crushed garlic

1 tsp chilli powder

1 tsp salt

½ tsp ground coriander

½ tsp ground cumin

4 tbsp sunflower oil

½ tsp onion seeds

½ tsp mustard seeds

½ tsp fenugreek seeds

pinch of white cumin seeds

3 dried red chillies

2 tbsp lemon juice

3 hard-boiled eggs

NUTRITION

Calories 170	Sugars 3g
Protein 6g	Fat 15g
Carbohydrate 3g	Saturates 2g

1 Place the tomatoes in a large bowl. Add the ginger, garlic, chilli powder, salt, ground coriander and ground cumin and blend well.

2 Heat the oil in a saucepan. Add the onion, mustard, fenugreek and white cumin seeds, and the dried red chillies, and stir-fry for 1 minute, or until they give off their aroma. Remove the saucepan from the heat.

3 Add the tomato mixture to the spicy oil mixture and return the pan to the heat. Stir-fry for 3 minutes.

4 Reduce the heat and continue to cook, partially covered, stirring frequently, for 7–10 minutes.

5 Sprinkle over 1 tablespoon of the lemon juice. Taste, and add the remaining lemon juice if required.

6 Transfer the tomato curry to a warmed serving dish and keep warm until required.

7 Shell the hard-boiled eggs and cut them into quarters. Add them to the curry, pushing them in gently, yolk-end down. Serve immediately.

creamy stuffed mushrooms

serves four

25 g/1 oz dried ceps

225 g/8 oz floury potatoes, diced

salt and pepper

2 tbsp butter, melted

4 tbsp double cream

2 tbsp snipped fresh chives

8 large open-cap mushrooms

25 g/1 oz Emmenthal cheese,
    grated

150 ml/5 fl oz vegetable stock

fresh chives, to garnish

salad leaves, to serve

1 Preheat the oven to 220°C/425°F/ Gas Mark 7. Place the dried ceps in a small bowl. Pour over enough boiling water to cover and leave to soak for 20 minutes.

2 Meanwhile, cook the potatoes in a saucepan of lightly salted boiling water for 10 minutes, or until cooked through and tender. Drain them well and mash until smooth.

3 Drain the soaked ceps and chop them finely. Mix them into the mashed potato.

4 Thoroughly blend the butter, cream and chives together and pour the mixture into the ceps and potato mixture, stirring well to blend. Season to taste with salt and pepper.

5 Remove the stalks from the open-cap mushrooms. Chop the stalks and stir them into the potato mixture. Spoon the mixture into the open-cap mushrooms and sprinkle the grated cheese over the top.

6 Arrange the filled mushrooms in a shallow ovenproof dish and pour the stock around them.

7 Cover the dish and cook in the preheated oven for 20 minutes. Remove the lid and cook for a further 5 minutes, or until the tops are golden.

8 Garnish the mushrooms with fresh chives and serve with salad leaves.

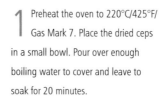

NUTRITION	
Calories 214	Sugars 1g
Protein 5g	Fat 17g
Carbohydrate 11g	Saturates 11g

broccoli in oyster sauce

serves four

250–300 g/9–10½ oz broccoli

3 tbsp vegetable oil

3–4 small slices fresh root ginger

½ tsp salt

½ tsp sugar

3–4 tbsp water

1 tbsp oyster sauce

NUTRITION

Calories 100	Sugars 1g
Protein 3g	Fat 9g
Carbohydrate 2g	Saturates 1g

COOK'S TIP

The broccoli stalks have to be peeled and cut diagonally to ensure that they will cook evenly. If they are thin stalks, the pieces can be added to the wok at the same time as the florets, but otherwise add the stalks first, to ensure that they will be tender.

1 Using a sharp knife, cut the broccoli spears into small florets. Trim the stalks, peel off the rough skin, and cut the stalks diagonally into diamond-shaped chunks.

2 Heat the oil in a preheated wok until really hot.

3 Add the pieces of broccoli stalk and the slices of ginger to the wok and stir-fry for 30 seconds, then add the florets and continue to stir-fry for a further 2 minutes.

4 Add the salt, sugar and water, and continue stirring for a further minute.

5 Blend in the oyster sauce. Transfer the broccoli to a serving dish and serve hot or cold.

spinach frittata

serves four

450 g/1 lb fresh spinach

2 tsp water

4 eggs, beaten

2 tbsp single cream

2 garlic cloves, crushed

55 g/2 oz canned sweetcorn
    kernels, drained

1 celery stick, chopped

1 fresh red chilli, deseeded
    and chopped

2 tomatoes, deseeded and diced

2 tbsp olive oil

2 tbsp butter

4 tbsp pecan nut halves

2 tbsp grated pecorino cheese

25 g/1 oz fontina cheese, cubed

pinch of paprika

COOK'S TIP

Be careful not to burn the
underside of the frittata during
the initial cooking stage – this is
why it is important to use a
heavy-based frying pan. Add a
little extra oil to the pan when
you turn the frittata over,
if required.

1 Cook the spinach in the water in a covered saucepan for 5 minutes. Drain thoroughly and pat dry on kitchen paper.

2 Beat the eggs in a bowl and stir in the spinach, cream, garlic, sweetcorn, celery, chilli and tomatoes until the ingredients are well mixed.

NUTRITION

Calories 307	Sugars 4g
Protein 15g	Fat 25g
Carbohydrate 6g	Saturates 8g

3 Heat the oil and butter in a 20-cm/8-inch heavy-based frying pan over a medium heat.

4 Spoon the egg mixture into the frying pan and sprinkle with the pecan nut halves, pecorino and fontina cheeses and paprika. Cook, without stirring, over a medium heat for 5–7 minutes, or until the underside of the frittata is brown.

5 Place a large plate over the frying pan and invert to turn out the frittata. Slide it back into the frying pan and cook the other side for a further 2–3 minutes. Serve the frittata straight from the frying pan or transfer to a serving plate and serve immediately.

ratatouille

serves four–six

1 large aubergine, about
  300 g/10½ oz

salt and pepper

5 tbsp olive oil

2 large onions, thinly sliced

2 large garlic cloves, crushed

4 courgettes, sliced

800 g/1 lb 12 oz canned
  chopped tomatoes

1 tsp sugar

1 bouquet garni of 2 fresh
  thyme sprigs, 2 large fresh
  parsley sprigs, 1 fresh basil sprig
  and 1 bay leaf, tied in a 7.5-cm/
  3-inch piece of celery

fresh basil leaves, to garnish

NUTRITION

Calories 157	Sugars 11g
Protein 4g	Fat 9g
Carbohydrate 14g	Saturates 1g

1 Roughly chop the aubergine, then place in a colander. Sprinkle with salt and leave to stand for 30 minutes to drain. Rinse well under cold running water to remove all traces of the salt and pat dry with kitchen paper.

2 Heat the oil in a large, heavy-based flameproof casserole over a medium heat. Add the onions, reduce the heat and cook, stirring occasionally, for 10 minutes, or until softened and light golden brown.

3 Add the garlic and continue to fry for 2 minutes, or until the onions are tender.

4 Add the aubergine, courgettes, tomatoes with their can juices, sugar and bouquet garni. Season to taste with salt and pepper. Bring to the boil, then reduce the heat to very low, cover and simmer for 30 minutes.

5 Taste and adjust the seasoning if necessary. Remove and discard the bouquet garni. Garnish the vegetable stew with basil leaves and serve immediately.

spinach & herb frittata

serves six–eight

4 tbsp olive oil

6 spring onions, sliced

250 g/9 oz young spinach
    leaves, any coarse stems
    removed, rinsed

6 large eggs

salt and pepper

3 tbsp finely chopped mixed fresh
    herbs, such as flat-leaf parsley,
    thyme and coriander

2 tbsp freshly grated Parmesan
    cheese, plus extra for garnishing

fresh parsley sprigs, to garnish

NUTRITION

Calories 145	Sugars 1g
Protein 8g	Fat 12g
Carbohydrate 1g	Saturates 13g

1 Preheat the grill. Heat a 25-cm/
10-inch frying pan, preferably
non-stick with a flameproof handle,
over a medium heat. Add the oil and
heat. Add the spring onions and cook
for 2 minutes.

2 Add the spinach and cook until it
is just wilted.

3 Beat the eggs and season to taste
with salt and pepper. Using a
slotted spoon, transfer the spinach and
onions to the eggs and stir in the herbs.
Pour the excess oil left in the frying pan
into a heatproof jug, then scrape off
the bits from the base of the pan.

4 Reheat the frying pan. Add
2 tablespoons of the reserved oil.
Pour in the egg mixture, smoothing it
into an even layer. Cook, shaking the
frying pan occasionally, for 6 minutes,
or until the base is set when you lift up
the side with a spatula.

5 Sprinkle the top of the frittata
with the Parmesan cheese. Place
the pan under the hot grill and cook for
3 minutes, or until the excess liquid is
set and the cheese is golden.

6 Remove the frying pan from the
heat and slide the frittata out
onto a warm serving plate. Leave the
frittata to stand for at least 5 minutes
before cutting and garnishing with
extra Parmesan cheese and parsley.
The frittata can be served hot, warm
or at room temperature.

thai-spiced mushrooms

serves four

8 large flat mushrooms

3 tbsp sunflower oil

2 tbsp light soy sauce

1 garlic clove, crushed

2-cm/¾-inch piece fresh galangal or
  root ginger, grated

1 tbsp Thai green curry paste

8 baby sweetcorn cobs, sliced

3 spring onions, chopped

125 g/4½ oz beansprouts

100 g/3½ oz firm tofu
  (drained weight), diced

2 tsp sesame seeds, toasted

TO SERVE

chopped cucumber

sliced red pepper

NUTRITION

Calories 147	Sugars 2g
Protein 6g	Fat 12g
Carbohydrate 4g	Saturates 1g

1 Preheat the grill to high. Remove the stalks from the mushrooms and reserve. Place the caps on a baking sheet. Mix 2 tablespoons of the oil with 1 tablespoon of the soy sauce and brush over the mushrooms.

2 Cook the mushroom caps under the hot grill until golden and tender, turning them over once.

3 Meanwhile, chop the mushroom stalks finely. Heat the remaining oil in a large frying pan or preheated wok. Add the stalks, garlic and galangal and stir-fry for 1 minute.

4 Stir in the curry paste, baby corn cobs and spring onions and stir-fry for 1 minute. Add the beansprouts and stir-fry for a further 1 minute.

5 Add the tofu and remaining soy sauce, then toss lightly to heat. Spoon the mixture into the mushroom caps.

6 Sprinkle with sesame seeds and serve with chopped cucumber and sliced red pepper.

vegetable rolls

serves four

8 large Chinese leaves

FILLING

2 baby sweetcorn cobs, sliced

1 carrot, finely chopped

1 celery stick, chopped

4 spring onions, chopped

4 water chestnuts, chopped

2 tbsp unsalted cashews, chopped

1 garlic clove, chopped

1 tsp grated fresh root ginger

25 g/1 oz canned bamboo shoots, drained, rinsed and chopped

1 tsp sesame oil

2 tsp soy sauce

NUTRITION	
Calories 69	Sugars 1g
Protein 2g	Fat 5g
Carbohydrate 3g	Saturates 1g

1 Place the Chinese leaves in a large bowl and pour over boiling water to soften them. Leave them to stand for 1 minute and drain thoroughly.

2 Mix the baby sweetcorn cobs, chopped carrot, celery, spring onions, water chestnuts, cashews, garlic, ginger and bamboo shoots together in a large bowl.

3 Whisk the sesame oil and soy sauce together in a separate bowl. Add this to the vegetables, and stir well until all the vegetables are thoroughly coated in the mixture.

4 Spread out the Chinese leaves on a chopping board and divide the filling mixture between them, carefully spooning an equal quantity of the mixture onto each leaf.

5 Roll up the Chinese leaves, folding in the sides, to make neat parcels. Secure the parcels with wooden cocktail sticks.

6 Place in a small heatproof dish in a steamer, cover and cook for 15–20 minutes, or until the parcels are cooked.

7 Transfer the vegetable rolls to a warmed serving dish and serve immediately.

Desserts

You can still enjoy a dessert or a sweet treat on a low-carbohydrate diet, as the following recipes prove. Some, of course, are higher in carbohydrates than others, so be sure to consult the nutritional information alongside each recipe when making your choice, so that you can limit the 'naughtier' ones to an occasional indulgence.

As with vegetables, eating as wide a variety of fruit as possible is the healthy approach, and here you can feast on luscious summer berries in Balsamic Strawberries (see page 216), fragrant tropical fruit in Pineapple with Tequila & Mint (see page 250) and no less enticing tree fruit in Peaches in White Wine (see page 234) and Poached Allspice Pears (see page 247).

But if a hit of chocolate is what you crave, try the sumptuous Mocha Swirl Mousse (see page 230) or the truly wicked Rich Chocolate Loaf (see page 218).

balsamic strawberries

serves four–six

450 g/1 lb fresh strawberries
2–3 tbsp balsamic vinegar
pepper
fresh mint leaves, torn, plus extra
   to decorate (optional)
115–175 g/4–6 oz mascarpone
   cheese

NUTRITION

Calories 132	Sugars 5g
Protein 1g	Fat 12g
Carbohydrate 5g	Saturates 7g

COOK'S TIP

This is most enjoyable when it is
made with the best quality
balsamic vinegar, one that has
aged slowly and has turned thick
and syrupy. Unfortunately, the
genuine mixture is always
expensive – cheaper versions are
artificially sweetened
and coloured.

1 Wipe the strawberries with a damp cloth, rather than rinsing them, so they do not become soggy. Using a paring knife, cut off the stalks at the top, then use the tip to remove the core.

2 Cut each strawberry in half or into quarters if large. Transfer to a large bowl.

3 Add ½ tablespoon of the vinegar per person. Add several twists of pepper, then gently stir together. Cover with clingfilm and leave to chill in the refrigerator for 4 hours.

4 Just before serving, stir in the mint leaves to taste. Spoon the mascarpone cheese into bowls and spoon the berries on top.

5 Decorate the balsamic strawberries with a few mint leaves, if wished. Sprinkle with extra pepper to taste.

rich chocolate loaf

makes sixteen slices

75 g/3 oz almonds

140 g/5 oz plain chocolate

6 tbsp unsalted butter

200 ml/7 fl oz condensed milk

2 tsp ground cinnamon

85 g/3 oz amaretti biscuits, broken

55 g/2 oz no-soak dried apricots,
  roughly chopped

NUTRITION	
Calories 118	Sugars 16g
Protein 3g	Fat 12g
Carbohydrate 18g	Saturates 6g

COOK'S TIP

To melt chocolate, first break
it into manageable pieces.
The smaller the pieces,
the quicker it will melt.

1 Line a 675-g/1-lb 8 oz loaf tin with a sheet of foil.

2 Using a sharp knife, roughly chop the almonds.

3 Place the plain chocolate, butter, condensed milk and cinnamon in a heavy-based saucepan.

4 Heat the chocolate mixture over a low heat for 3–4 minutes, stirring constantly with a wooden spoon, until the chocolate has melted. Beat the mixture well.

5 Stir the chopped almonds, broken biscuits and chopped apricots into the chocolate mixture, stirring with a wooden spoon until well mixed.

6 Pour the mixture into the prepared tin and leave to chill in the refrigerator for 1 hour, or until set. Cut the rich chocolate loaf into slices to serve.

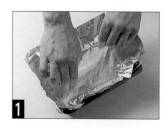

coconut sweet

NUTRITION	
Calories 338	Sugars 5g
Protein 4g	Fat 34g
Carbohydrate 5g	Saturates 26g

COOK'S TIP

Coconut is used extensively in Indian cooking to add flavour and creaminess to various dishes. The best flavour comes from freshly grated coconut, although ready-prepared desiccated coconut, as used here, makes an excellent standby. Freshly grated coconut freezes successfully, so it is well worth preparing when you have the time.

1 Place the butter in a heavy-based saucepan and melt over a low heat, stirring constantly.

2 Add the desiccated coconut to the melted butter, stirring to mix.

3 Stir in the condensed milk and the pink food colouring, if using, and mix constantly for 7–10 minutes.

4 Remove the saucepan from the heat and leave the coconut mixture to cool slightly.

5 Once cool enough to handle, shape the coconut mixture into long blocks and cut into equal-sized rectangles. Leave to set for 1 hour, then serve.

mini florentines

makes forty

6 tbsp butter, plus extra for greasing

plain flour, for dusting

75 g/2¾ oz caster sugar

2 tbsp sultanas or raisins

2 tbsp chopped glacé cherries

2 tbsp chopped crystallized ginger

25 g/1 oz sunflower seeds

100 g/3½ oz flaked almonds

2 tbsp double cream

175 g/6 oz plain chocolate

NUTRITION

Calories 75	Sugars 6g
Protein 1g	Fat 5g
Carbohydrate 6g	Saturates 2g

1 Preheat the oven to 180°C/
350°F/Gas Mark 4. Grease and
flour 2 baking sheets.

2 Place the remaining butter in a
saucepan and heat until melted.
Add the sugar, stir until dissolved, then
bring to the boil. Remove from the
heat and stir in the sultanas, cherries,
ginger, sunflower seeds and almonds.
Mix well, then beat in the cream.

3 Place small teaspoons of the
fruit and nut mixture onto the
prepared baking sheets, allowing
plenty of space for the mixture to
spread. Bake in the preheated oven for
10–12 minutes, or until light golden.

4 Remove from the oven and, while
still hot, use a circular biscuit
cutter to pull in the edges to form
perfect circles. Leave to cool and go
crisp before removing from the
baking sheets.

5 Break the chocolate into pieces,
place in a heatproof bowl over a
saucepan of simmering water and stir
until melted. Spread most of the
chocolate onto a sheet of baking paper.
When the chocolate is on the point of
setting, place the biscuits flat-side
down on the chocolate and let it
harden completely.

6 Cut around the florentines and
remove from the baking paper.
Spread a little more melted chocolate
on the coated side of the florentines
and use a fork to mark waves in the
chocolate. Leave to set. Arrange the
florentines on a plate (or in a
presentation box for a gift) with
alternate sides facing upwards. Keep
them cool.

lavender hearts

makes about forty-eight

225 g/8 oz plain flour, plus extra
    for dusting

75 g/2¾ oz chilled butter, diced

75 g/2¾ oz caster sugar

1 large egg

1 tbsp dried lavender flowers, very
    finely chopped

TO DECORATE

about 4 tbsp icing sugar

about 1 tsp cold water

about 2 tbsp fresh lavender flowers

NUTRITION

Calories 36	Sugars 2g
Protein 1g	Fat 1g
Carbohydrate 5g	Saturates 1g

1 Preheat the oven to 180°C/350°F/
Gas Mark 4. Line 2 baking sheets
with baking paper. Place the flour in a
bowl, add the butter and rub it in until
the mixture resembles crumbs. Stir in
the sugar.

2 Lightly beat the egg, then add it
to the flour and butter mixture
along with the dried lavender flowers.
Stir the mixture until a stiff paste
is formed.

3 Turn out the dough onto a lightly
floured work surface and roll out
until about 5 mm/¼ inch thick.

4 Using a 5-cm/2-inch heart-shaped
biscuit cutter, press out
48 biscuits, occasionally dipping the
cutter into extra flour, and re-rolling the
trimmings as necessary. Transfer the
pastry hearts to the baking sheets.

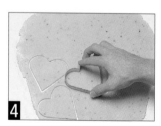

5 Prick the surface of each heart
with a fork. Bake in the preheated
oven for 10 minutes, or until lightly
browned. Transfer to a wire rack set
over a sheet of baking paper to cool.

6 Sift the icing sugar into a bowl.
Add the water and stir until a
thin, smooth icing forms, adding a little
extra water if necessary.

7 Drizzle the icing from the tip of
the spoon over the cooled biscuits
in a random pattern. Immediately
sprinkle with the fresh lavender flowers
while the icing is still soft so that they
stick in place. Leave for at least
15 minutes, or until the icing has set.
Store the biscuits for up to 4 days in an
airtight container.

zabaglione

serves six

4 egg yolks

70 g/2½ oz caster sugar

125 ml/4 fl oz Marsala wine

amaretti biscuits, to serve (optional)

NUTRITION

Calories 110	Sugars 13g
Protein 2g	Fat 4g
Carbohydrate 13g	Saturates 1g

COOK'S TIP

Decorate the zabaglione
with a slit strawberry, placed on
the rim of the glass, or serve
with sponge fingers
or crisp biscuits.

1 Half-fill a saucepan with water and bring to the boil. Reduce the heat so that the water is barely simmering.

2 Whisk the egg yolks and sugar together in a heatproof bowl with an electric whisk until pale and creamy. Set the bowl over the saucepan of water. Do not let the base touch the surface of the water, or the egg yolks will scramble.

3 Gradually add the Marsala wine, whisking constantly with the electric whisk. Continue whisking until the mixture is thick and has increased in volume. Pour into heatproof glasses or bowls and serve immediately with amaretti biscuits, if using.

italian chocolate truffles

makes twenty four

175 g/6 oz plain chocolate

2 tbsp almond-flavoured liqueur or
   orange-flavoured liqueur

40 g/1½ oz unsalted butter

50 g/1¾ oz icing sugar

50 g/1¾ oz ground almonds

50 g/1¾ oz milk chocolate, grated

NUTRITION	
Calories 82	Sugars 7g
Protein 1g	Fat 5g
Carbohydrate 8g	Saturates 3g

1 Melt the plain chocolate with the liqueur in a bowl set over a saucepan of hot water, stirring until well combined.

2 Add the butter and stir until it has melted. Stir in the icing sugar and the ground almonds.

3 Leave the mixture in a cool place until firm enough to roll into 24 balls.

4 Place the grated milk chocolate on a plate and roll the truffles in the chocolate to coat them.

5 Place the truffles in paper sweet cases and leave to chill.

VARIATION

Almond-flavoured liqueur gives these truffles an authentic Italian flavour. The original almond liqueur, Amaretto di Saronno, comes from Saronno in Italy.

exotic fruit parcels

serves four

1 papaya

1 mango

1 star fruit

1 tbsp grenadine

3 tbsp orange juice

low-fat natural yogurt or single
    cream, to serve

NUTRITION

Calories 43	Sugars 9g
Protein 2g	Fat 0.3g
Carbohydrate 9g	Saturates 0.1g

1 Cut the papaya in half, scoop out the seeds and discard them. Peel the papaya and cut the flesh into thick slices.

2 Prepare the mango by cutting it in half lengthways and cutting carefully away from the flat central stone with a sharp knife.

3 Score each mango half in a criss-cross pattern. Push each mango half inside out to separate the cubes and cut them away from the peel.

4 Using a sharp knife, thickly slice the star fruit.

5 Place all of the fruit in a bowl and mix them together.

6 Mix the grenadine and orange juice together and pour over the fruit. Leave to marinate for at least 30 minutes.

7 Preheat the barbecue. Divide the fruit between 4 double thickness squares of foil and gather up the edges to form a parcel that encloses the fruit.

8 Place the foil parcels on a rack set over warm coals and barbecue the fruit for 15–20 minutes.

9 Serve the fruit in its parcel, with the natural yogurt.

rose ice

serves four

400 ml/14 fl oz water

2 tbsp coconut cream

4 tbsp sweetened condensed milk

2 tsp rosewater

few drops pink food colouring
(optional)

pink rose petals, to decorate

NUTRITION

Calories 76	Sugars 9g
Protein 2g	Fat 4g
Carbohydrate 9g	Saturates 3g

COOK'S TIP

To prevent the ice thawing too quickly at the table, nestle the base of the serving dish in another dish filled with crushed ice.

1 Place the water in a small saucepan and add the coconut cream. Heat the mixture gently without boiling, stirring constantly.

2 Remove from the heat and leave to cool. Stir in the sweetened condensed milk, rosewater and food colouring, if using.

3 Pour into a freezerproof container and freeze for 1–1½ hours, or until slushy.

4 Remove from the freezer and break up the ice crystals with a fork. Return to the freezer and freeze until firm.

5 Spoon the ice roughly into a pile on a serving dish and sprinkle with rose petals to serve.

mocha swirl mousse

serves four

1 tbsp coffee and chicory essence

2 tsp cocoa powder, plus extra
    for dusting

1 tsp low-fat drinking
    chocolate powder

150 ml/5 fl oz low-fat crème fraîche,
    plus 4 tsp to serve

2 tsp powdered gelozone
    (vegetarian gelatine)

2 tbsp boiling water

2 large egg whites

2 tbsp caster sugar

4 chocolate coffee beans, to serve

NUTRITION

Calories 136	Sugars 5g
Protein 5g	Fat 8g
Carbohydrate 11g	Saturates 5g

COOK'S TIP

The vegetarian equivalent of
gelatine, called gelozone, is
available from healthfood shops.

1 Place the coffee and chicory essence in one bowl, and 2 teaspoons cocoa powder and the drinking chocolate in another bowl. Divide the crème fraîche between the 2 bowls and mix both well.

2 Dissolve the gelozone in the boiling water and reserve. Whisk the egg whites and sugar in a greasefree bowl until stiff and divide this evenly between the 2 mixtures.

3 Divide the dissolved gelozone between the 2 mixtures and, using a large metal spoon, gently fold until well mixed.

4 Spoon small amounts of the 2 mousses alternately into 4 serving glasses and swirl together gently. Place in the refrigerator and leave to chill for 1 hour, or until set.

5 To serve, top each mousse with a teaspoonful of reserved crème fraîche, a chocolate coffee bean and a light dusting of cocoa powder. Serve.

figs with orange cream

serves four

8 large fresh figs
4 large fresh fig leaves, if available,
    rinsed and dried
CREME FRAICHE (OPTIONAL)
2 tbsp buttermilk
300 ml/10 fl oz double cream
ORANGE BLOSSOM CREAM
125 ml/4 fl oz crème fraîche,
    home-made or shop-bought
about 4 tbsp orange blossom water
1 tsp orange blossom honey
finely grated rind of ½ orange
2 tbsp flaked almonds, to
    decorate (optional)

1 If you are making the Crème
Fraîche, begin at least a day
ahead. Place the buttermilk in a
preserving jar or a jar with a screw top.
Add the cream, close securely and
shake to blend. Leave to stand at room
temperature for 6–8 hours, or until set,
then chill for at least 8 hours and up to
4 days. It will develop a slight tangy
flavour. Lightly beat before using.

2 To toast the almonds for the
decoration, place in a dry frying
pan over a medium heat and stir until
lightly browned. Take care that they do
not burn. Immediately tip the almonds
out of the frying pan. Reserve.

3 To make the Orange Blossom
Cream, place the crème fraîche in
a small bowl and stir in the orange
blossom water with the orange
blossom honey and orange rind. Taste
and add a little extra orange blossom
water if necessary.

4 To serve, cut the stems off the
figs, but do not peel them. Stand
the figs upright with the pointed end
upwards. Cut each into quarters
without cutting all the way through,
so you can open them out into
attractive 'flowers'.

5 If you are using fig leaves, place
one in the centre of each serving
plate. Arrange 2 figs on top of each
leaf, and spoon a small amount of the
orange-flavoured cream alongside
them. Sprinkle the cream with the
toasted flaked almonds if desired,
just before serving.

NUTRITION	
Calories 20	Sugars 13g
Protein 3g	Fat 18g
Carbohydrate 14g	Saturates 9g

paper-thin fruit pies

serves four

1 dessert apple

1 ripe pear

2 tbsp lemon juice

55 g/2 oz low-fat spread

225 g/8 oz filo pastry, thawed
   if frozen

2 tbsp low-sugar apricot jam

1 tbsp unsweetened orange juice

1 tbsp finely chopped pistachio nuts

2 tsp icing sugar, for dusting

low-fat custard, to serve

NUTRITION

Calories 158	Sugars 12g
Protein 2g	Fat 10g
Carbohydrate 14g	Saturates 2g

1 Preheat the oven to 200°C/400°F/
Gas Mark 6. Core and thinly slice
the apple and pear and toss them in
the lemon juice.

VARIATION

Other combinations of fruit are
equally delicious. Try peach and
apricot, raspberry and apple or
pineapple and mango.

2 Melt the low-fat spread in a small
saucepan over a low heat. Cut
the sheets of pastry into 4 and cover
with a clean, damp tea towel. Brush
4 non-stick shallow tins, measuring
10 cm/4 inches across, with a little of
the low-fat spread.

3 Working on each pie separately,
brush 4 sheets of pastry with low-
fat spread. Press a small sheet of pastry
into the base of one tin. Arrange the
other sheets of pastry on top at slightly
different angles. Repeat with the
remaining sheets of pastry to make
another 3 pies. Arrange the apple and
pear slices alternately in the centre of
each pastry case and lightly crimp the
edges of the pastry of each pie.

4 Mix the jam and orange juice
together until smooth and brush
over the fruit. Bake in the preheated
oven for 12–15 minutes. Sprinkle with
the pistachio nuts, dust lightly with
icing sugar and serve with custard.

peaches in white wine

serves four

4 large peaches

2 tbsp icing sugar, sifted

1 orange

200 ml/7 fl oz medium or sweet
white wine, chilled

NUTRITION

Calories 89	Sugars 14g
Protein 1g	Fat 0g
Carbohydrate 14g	Saturates 0g

COOK'S TIP

There is absolutely no need to
use expensive wine in this recipe,
so it can be quite economical
to make.

1 Using a sharp knife, halve the peaches, remove the stones and discard them. Peel the peaches, if you prefer. Slice into thin wedges.

2 Place the peach wedges in a glass serving bowl and sprinkle over the icing sugar.

3 Using a sharp knife, pare the rind from the orange. Cut the orange rind into matchsticks, place them in a bowl of cold water and reserve.

4 Squeeze the juice from the orange and pour over the peaches, together with the chilled white wine.

5 Place the bowl in the refrigerator for at least 1 hour to allow the peaches to marinate and chill.

6 Remove the orange rind matchsticks from the water and pat them dry with kitchen paper.

7 Decorate the chilled marinated peaches with the strips of orange rind and serve immediately.

tropical salad

serves eight

1 papaya

2 tbsp fresh orange juice

3 tbsp rum

2 bananas

2 guavas

1 small pineapple or 2 baby
   pineapples

2 passion fruit

pineapple leaves to decorate

NUTRITION

Calories 69	Sugars 13g
Protein 1g	Fat 0.3g
Carbohydrate 14g	Saturates 0g

COOK'S TIP

Guavas have a heavenly smell
when ripe – their scent will fill a
whole room. They should give to
gentle pressure when ripe, and
their skins should be yellow. The
canned varieties are very good
and have a pink tinge to
the flesh.

1 Cut the papaya in half and remove and discard the seeds. Peel and slice the flesh into a bowl.

2 Pour over the orange juice together with the rum.

3 Peel and slice the bananas and peel and slice the guavas, then add both to the bowl.

4 Cut the top and base from the pineapple, then cut off the skin.

5 Slice the pineapple flesh, discard the core, cut into pieces and add to the bowl.

6 Halve the passion fruit, scoop out the flesh with a teaspoon, add to the bowl and stir well to mix.

7 Spoon the salad into glass bowls and decorate with pineapple leaves. Serve.

chocolate biscotti

makes sixteen

butter, for greasing

1 egg

100 g/3½ oz caster sugar

1 tsp vanilla essence

125 g/4½ oz plain flour, plus extra
  for dusting

½ tsp baking powder

1 tsp ground cinnamon

50 g/1¾ oz plain chocolate,
  roughly chopped

50 g/1¾ oz toasted flaked almonds

50 g/1¾ oz pine kernels

NUTRITION

Calories 113	Sugars 9g
Protein 2g	Fat 5g
Carbohydrate 15g	Saturates 1g

1 Preheat the oven to 180°C/350°F/
Gas Mark 4. Grease a baking tray
with butter. Reserve.

2 Whisk the egg, sugar and vanilla
essence in a large bowl with an
electric mixer until it is thick and pale –
ribbons of mixture should trail from the
whisk as you lift it.

3 Sift the flour, baking powder and
cinnamon into a separate bowl,
then sift into the egg mixture and
fold in gently. Stir in the plain
chocolate, flaked almonds and
pine kernels.

4 Turn out onto a floured work
surface and shape into a flat log,
23 cm/9 inches long and 2 cm/¾ inch
wide. Transfer to the baking tray.

5 Bake in the preheated oven for
20–25 minutes, or until golden.
Remove from the oven and leave to
cool for 5 minutes, or until firm.

6 Transfer the log to a chopping
board. Using a serrated bread
knife, cut the log on the diagonal into
slices about 1 cm/½ inch thick and
arrange them on the baking tray. Cook
for 10–15 minutes, turning halfway
through the cooking time.

7 Cool for 5 minutes. Transfer to a
wire rack to cool completely.

creamy fruit parfait

serves four–six

225 g/8 oz cherries

2 large peaches

2 large apricots

700 ml/1¼ pints Greek-style yogurt
or natural thick yogurt

55 g/2 oz walnut halves

2 tbsp flower-scented honey

fresh redcurrants or berries, to
decorate (optional)

NUTRITION

Calories 261		Sugars 17g	
Protein 10g		Fat 18g	
Carbohydrate 17g		Saturates 7g	

1 To prepare the fruit, use a cherry or olive stoner to remove the cherry stones. Cut each cherry in half. Cut the peaches and apricots in half from top to bottom and remove the stones, then finely chop the flesh of all the fruit.

2 Place the finely chopped cherries, peaches and apricots in a bowl and gently stir together.

3 Spoon one-third of the yogurt into an attractive glass serving bowl. Top with half the fruit mixture.

4 Repeat with another layer of yogurt and fruit and, finally, top with the remaining yogurt.

5 Place the walnuts in a small food processor and pulse until they are chopped into quite small pieces, but not finely ground. Alternatively, chop them with a sharp knife. Sprinkle the walnuts over the top of the yogurt.

6 Drizzle the honey over the nuts and yogurt. Cover with clingfilm and leave to chill in the refrigerator for at least 1 hour. Decorate the bowl with a small bunch of fresh redcurrants, if using, just before serving.

lemon & lime syllabub

serves four

50 g/1¾ oz caster sugar

grated rind and juice of
1 small lemon

grated rind and juice of 1 small lime

50 ml/2 fl oz Marsala or
medium sherry

300 ml/10 fl oz double cream

lime and lemon zest, to decorate

NUTRITION

Calories 403	Sugars 16g
Protein 2g	Fat 36g
Carbohydrate 16g	Saturates 22g

1 Place the sugar, fruit juices and rind and Marsala in a bowl. Mix well and leave to infuse for 2 hours.

2 Add the cream to the mixture and whisk until it just holds its shape.

3 Spoon the mixture into 4 tall serving glasses and leave to chill in the refrigerator for 2 hours.

4 Decorate with lime and lemon zest and serve.

COOK'S TIP

Do not overwhip the cream when adding to the lemon and lime mixture because it may curdle. Replace the double cream with natural yogurt for a healthier version of this dessert, or use half quantities of both. Whisk the cream before adding to the yogurt.

VARIATION

For an alternative citrus flavour, substitute 2 oranges for the lemon and lime, if you prefer.

lime mousse with mango

serves four

250 g/9 oz fromage frais

grated rind of 1 lime

1 tbsp caster sugar

125 ml/4 fl oz double cream

MANGO SAUCE

1 mango

juice of 1 lime

4 tsp caster sugar

TO DECORATE

4 cape gooseberries

strips of lime rind

NUTRITION

Calories 254	Sugars 17g
Protein 5g	Fat 19g
Carbohydrate 17g	Saturates 12g

COOK'S TIP

Cape gooseberries have a tart and mildly scented flavour and make an excellent decoration for many desserts. Peel back the papery husks to expose the bright orange fruits.

1 Place the fromage frais, lime rind and sugar in a large bowl and mix together.

2 Whisk the double cream in a separate bowl and fold into the fromage frais.

3 Line 4 decorative moulds or ramekin dishes with muslin or clingfilm and divide the mixture evenly between them. Fold the muslin or clingfilm over the top and press down firmly. Leave to chill for 30 minutes.

4 To make the sauce, slice through the mango on each side of the large flat stone, then cut the flesh from the stone. Remove the skin.

5 Cut off 12 thin slices and reserve. Chop the remaining mango and place in a food processor with the lime juice and sugar. Blend until smooth. Alternatively, push the mango through a sieve, then mix with the lime juice and sugar.

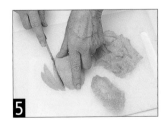

6 Turn the moulds out onto serving plates. Arrange 3 slices of mango on each plate, pour some sauce around, decorate and serve.

melon & kiwi salad

serves four

½ Galia melon

2 kiwi fruits

125 g/4½ oz white seedless grapes

1 papaya, halved

3 tbsp orange-flavoured liqueur,
   such as Cointreau

1 tbsp chopped fresh lemon
   verbena, lemon balm or mint

TO DECORATE

fresh lemon verbena sprigs

cape gooseberries

NUTRITION

Calories 88	Sugars 17g
Protein 1g	Fat 0.2g
Carbohydrate 17g	Saturates 0g

1 Remove the seeds from the melon, cut it into 4 slices and carefully cut away the skin. Cut the flesh into cubes and place in a bowl.

2 Peel the kiwi fruits and cut across into slices. Add to the melon with the white grapes.

3 Remove the seeds from the papaya and cut off the skin. Slice the flesh thickly and cut into diagonal pieces. Add to the fruit bowl and mix well.

4 Mix the liqueur and the chopped lemon verbena together, pour over the fruit and leave to macerate for 1 hour, stirring occasionally.

5 Spoon the fruit salad into a glass bowl, pour over the juices and decorate with lemon verbena sprigs and cape gooseberries.

COOK'S TIP

Lemon balm or sweet balm is a fragrant lemon-scented plant with slightly hairy serrated leaves and a pronounced lemon flavour. Lemon verbena can also be used – this has an even stronger lemon flavour and smooth elongated leaves.

mini frangipane tartlets with lime

makes twelve

125 g/4½ oz plain flour, plus extra
  for dusting

100 g/3½ oz butter, softened

1 tsp grated lime rind

1 tbsp lime juice

50 g/1¾ oz caster sugar

1 egg

25 g/1 oz ground almonds

50 g/1¾ oz icing sugar, sifted

½ tbsp water

1 Preheat the oven to 200°C/400°F/
Gas Mark 6. Reserve 5 teaspoons
of the flour and 3 teaspoons of
the butter.

2 Rub the remaining butter into the
remaining flour until the mixture
resembles fine breadcrumbs. Stir in the
lime rind, followed by the lime juice,
then bring the mixture together with
your fingers to form a soft dough.

3 Roll out the dough thinly on a
floured work surface. Stamp out
12 rounds, 7.5 cm/3 inches wide, with
a fluted cutter, and line a bun tin.

4 Cream the reserved butter and
the caster sugar together in a
large bowl.

5 Mix in the egg, then the ground
almonds and the reserved flour.

6 Divide the almond mixture
between the pastry cases.

7 Bake in the preheated oven for
15 minutes, or until set and
lightly golden. Turn the tartlets out
onto a wire rack to cool.

8 Mix the icing sugar with the
water. Drizzle a little of the icing
over each tartlet and serve.

NUTRITION	
Calories 149	Sugars 9g
Protein 2g	Fat 9g
Carbohydrate 17g	Saturates 5g

pink syllabubs

serves two

5 tbsp white wine

2–3 tsp blackcurrant liqueur

finely grated rind of ½ lemon

    or orange

1 tbsp caster sugar

200 ml/7 fl oz double cream

TO DECORATE

fresh fruit, such as strawberries,

    raspberries or redcurrants,

    or pecan or walnut halves

fresh mint sprigs

NUTRITION

Calories 536	Sugars 17g
Protein 2g	Fat 48g
Carbohydrate 17g	Saturates 30g

COOK'S TIP

These syllabubs will keep in the refrigerator for 48 hours, so it is worth making more than you need and keeping the extra for another day.

1 Mix the white wine, blackcurrant liqueur, grated lemon rind and caster sugar together in a bowl and leave to stand for at least 30 minutes.

2 Add the cream to the wine mixture and whip until the mixture has thickened enough to stand in soft peaks.

3 If you desire, place some slices or small pieces of the fresh fruit or nuts in the bottom of 2 glasses. Place the cream and wine mixture into a piping bag fitted with a large star or plain nozzle and pipe into two glasses (over the fruit, if using). Alternatively, simply pour the syllabub into the glasses. Chill in the refrigerator until ready to serve.

4 Before serving, decorate each syllabub with the remaining pieces of fresh soft fruit or nuts, and mint sprigs.

chinese-style poached allspice pears

serves four

4 large ripe pears

300 ml/10 fl oz orange juice

2 tsp ground allspice

55 g/2 oz raisins

2 tbsp light brown sugar

grated orange rind, to decorate

COOK'S TIP

The Chinese do not usually have desserts to finish off a meal, except at banquets and special occasions. Sweet dishes are usually served in between main meals as snacks, but fruit is refreshing at the end of a big meal.

1 Using an apple corer, core the pears. Using a sharp knife, peel the pears and cut them in half.

2 Place the pear halves in a large heavy-based saucepan.

3 Add the orange juice, allspice, raisins and sugar to the saucepan and heat gently, stirring, or until the sugar has dissolved. Bring the mixture to the boil for 1 minute.

NUTRITION	
Calories 157	Sugars 17g
Protein 5g	Fat 19g
Carbohydrate 17g	Saturates 12g

4 Reduce the heat to low and leave to simmer for 10 minutes, or until the pears are cooked, but still fairly firm – test them by inserting the tip of a small sharp knife.

5 Remove the cooked pears from the saucepan with a slotted spoon and transfer to serving plates. Decorate with the grated orange rind and serve hot with the syrup.

247

chocolate cheese pots

serves four

300 ml/10 fl oz low-fat natural
    fromage frais

150 ml/5 fl oz low-fat natural yogurt

2 tbsp icing sugar

4 tsp low-fat drinking
    chocolate powder

4 tsp cocoa powder

1 tsp vanilla essence

2 tbsp dark rum (optional)

2 egg whites

4 chocolate cake decorations,
    to decorate

assorted fruit, such as pieces of
    kiwi fruit, orange, strawberries
    and raspberries, to serve

NUTRITION

Calories 117	Sugars 17g
Protein 9g	Fat 1g
Carbohydrate 18g	Saturates 1g

1 Mix the fromage frais and yogurt together in a bowl. Sift in the icing sugar, drinking chocolate and cocoa powder and mix well. Add the vanilla essence and rum, if using.

2 Whisk the egg whites in a clean bowl until stiff. Using a metal spoon, gently fold the egg whites into the chocolate mixture.

3 Spoon the fromage frais and chocolate mixture into 4 small china dessert pots and leave to chill in the refrigerator for 30 minutes.

4 Decorate each chocolate cheese pot with a chocolate decoration and serve with an assortment of fresh fruit, such as kiwi fruit, orange, strawberries and raspberries.

COOK'S TIP

This mixture would make an excellent filling for a cheesecake. Make the base out of crushed amaretti biscuits and egg white, and set the filling with 2 tbsp gelozone dissolved in 2 tbsp of boiling water.

pineapple with tequila & mint

serves four–six

1 ripe pineapple

sugar, to taste

juice of 1 lemon

2–3 tbsp tequila or a few drops of
vanilla essence

several fresh mint sprigs, leaves
removed and cut into thin strips

fresh mint sprig, to decorate

NUTRITION

Calories 87	Sugars 19g
Protein 1g	Fat 0g
Carbohydrate 19g	Saturates 0g

COOK'S TIP

Make sure you slice off the 'eyes'
when removing the skin from
the pineapple.

1 Using a sharp knife, cut off the top and bottom of the pineapple. Place upright on a board, then slice off the skin, cutting downwards. Cut in half, remove the core if wished, then cut the flesh into chunks.

2 Place the pineapple in a bowl and sprinkle with the sugar, lemon juice and tequila.

3 Toss the pineapple to coat well, then cover and leave to chill until ready to serve.

4 To serve, arrange on a large serving plate and sprinkle with the mint strips. Decorate the dish with a mint sprig.

VARIATION

Substitute 3 peeled sliced
mangoes for the pineapple. To
prepare mango, slice off a large
piece of flesh on either side of
the stone, peel and cut into
chunks. Slice off the remaining
flesh attached to the stone.

raspberry fool

serves four

300 g/10½ oz fresh raspberries

50 g/1¾ oz icing sugar

300 ml/10 fl oz crème fraîche

½ tsp vanilla essence

2 egg whites

TO DECORATE

fresh raspberries

lemon balm leaves

NUTRITION

Calories 288	Sugars 19g
Protein 4g	Fat 22g
Carbohydrate 19g	Saturates 14g

COOK'S TIP

Although this dessert is best made with fresh raspberries, an acceptable result can be achieved with frozen raspberries, available from supermarkets.

1 Place the raspberries and icing sugar in a food processor or blender and process until smooth. Alternatively, press through a sieve with the back of a spoon.

2 Reserve 4 tablespoons of crème fraîche for decorating.

3 Place the vanilla essence and remaining crème fraîche in a bowl and stir in the raspberry mixture.

4 Whisk the egg whites in a separate mixing bowl until stiff peaks form. Gently fold the egg whites into the raspberry mixture using a metal spoon, or until fully incorporated.

5 Spoon the raspberry fool into serving dishes and leave to chill for at least 1 hour. Decorate with the reserved crème fraîche, raspberries and lemon balm leaves and serve.